by John McPhee

THE
SURVIVAL
OF THE
BARK
CANOE

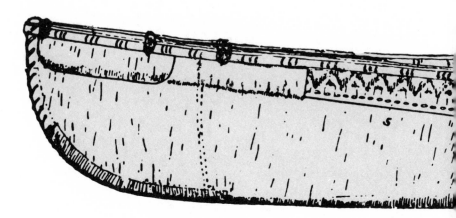

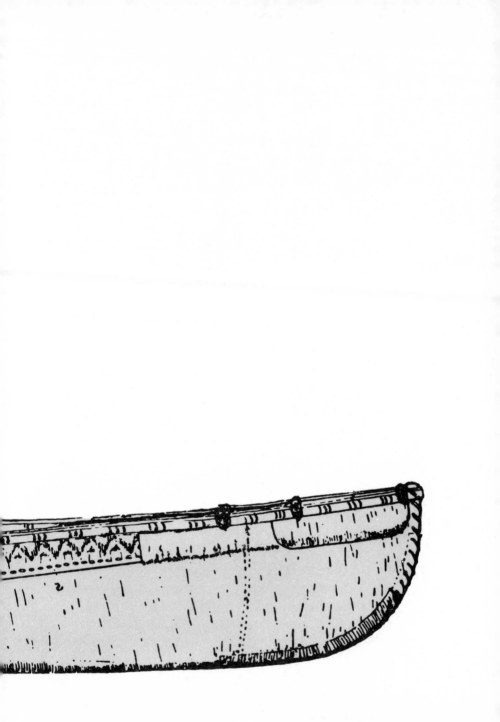

THE
SURVIVAL
OF THE
BARK
CANOE

JOHN
McPHEE

Farrar, Straus and Giroux
New York

Library of Congress Cataloging-in-Publication Data
McPhee, John A. / The survival of the bark canoe.
1. Canoes and canoeing—Maine.
2. Vaillancourt, Henri. I. Title.
VM353.M28   623.8'12'9   75-26558

The contents of this book, except "A Portfolio of the
Sketches and Models of Edwin Tappan Adney (1868–1950),"
originally appeared in The New Yorker, and were
developed with the editorial counsel of
William Shawn, Robert Bingham,
and C. P. Crow.

TO JOHN KAUFFMANN

CONTENTS

THE
SURVIVAL
OF THE
BARK
CANOE

When Henri Vaillancourt goes off to the Maine woods, he does not make extensive plans. Plans annoy him. He just gets out his pack baskets, tosses in some food and gear, takes a canoe, and goes. He makes (in advance) his own beef jerky—slow-baking for many hours the leanest beef he can find. He takes some oatmeal, some honey, some peanut butter. Not being sure how long he will be gone, he makes only a guess at how much food he may need, although he is going into the Penobscot-Allagash wilderness, north of Moosehead Lake. He takes no utensils. He prefers to carve them. He makes his own tumplines, his own carry boards. He makes his own paddles. They have slender blades, no more than five inches across. He roughs them out with his axe and carves them with his crooked knife, a tool well known in the north woods, almost unknown everywhere else. And—his primary function—he makes his own canoes. He carves their thwarts from hardwood and their ribs from cedar. He sews them and lashes them with the split roots of white pine. There are no nails, screws, or rivets keeping his canoes together—just the root lashings, in groups spaced handsomely along the gunwales, holding the framework to the bark.

Vaillancourt built his first canoe in 1965, when he was fifteen. He had tried to make other canoes in earlier years, always working by trial and error, until error prevailed. He had never paddled a canoe, had not so much as had a ride in one. In a passionate way, he had become interested in Indian life, and the aspect of it that most attracted him was the means by which the Indians had moved so easily on lakes and streams through otherwise detentive forests. He wanted to feel—if only approximately—what that had been like. His desire to do so became a preoccupation. He has said that he would have settled gladly for a ride in a wood-and-canvas canoe, or even an aluminum or a Fiberglas canoe—any canoe at all. But no one he knew had one. His town—Greenville, in southern New Hampshire—was small and had suffered from closing mills and regional depression. Greenville had ponds but no canoes. So far as he could see, there was only one way to achieve his wish. If he wanted to ride in a canoe, he would have to make one, and from materials at hand. White birches were all through the woods around the town. After his first couple of failures, a cousin who had become aware of his compulsion sent him an old copy of *Sports Afield* in which an article described, without much detail, how the Indians had done it. Henri laid out a building bed, went out and cut bark and saplings, and began to grope his way into a technology that had evolved in the forest under anonymous hands and—as he would learn—was much too complex merely to be called ingenious. His standards were—where else?—in their nascent stages, and he made his ribs out of unsplit saplings. What came up off the bed, though, was a finished, symmetrical, classical canoe. He picked it up and took it to a pond. He is lyrical (uncharacteristically lyrical) in describing that moment in that day and the feel of the canoe's momentum and response. "The first canoe I ever got into was one of my own. I can launch the best ones now and they don't thrill me one-tenth as much. It was the glide, the feel of it, just the sound as it rustled over the lily pads."

He took the canoe home and, before long, destroyed it with an axe. "It was a piece of junk," he explains. "I didn't want it around to embarrass me. Pieces of it still crop up here, now and then, and they go into the stove." He had had his initial thrill, and it had felt good, but his standards had gone shooting skyward, and that first canoe would never do. He formed an ambition, which he still has, to make a perfect bark canoe, and he says he will not rest until he has done so. He says that some of his canoes may look perfect to other people but they don't to him, because he sees things other people cannot discern. He has built thirty-three birch-bark canoes. He is in his mid-twenties now, and—with the snowshoes and paddles he makes in winter—he does nothing else for a living. Three or four Indians in Canada are also professional makers of bark canoes, and one old white man in Minnesota. All the rest—the centuries of them—are dead. With a singleness of purpose that defeats distraction, Henri Vaillancourt has appointed himself the keeper of this art. He has visited almost all the other living bark-canoe makers, and he has learned certain things from the Indians. He has returned home believing, though, that he is the most skillful of them all.

What he learned from the Indians was minor detail, such as using square pegs instead of round ones to secure his gunwale caps. His actual teacher (through the printed sketch and the printed word) was Edwin Tappan Adney, who died in the year that Vaillancourt was born. Without Adney, Vaillancourt might today be working in a plastics factory. Adney was an American who went to New Brunswick in the eighteen-eighties and built a bark canoe under the guidance of a Malecite. He was twenty, and he recorded everything the Malecite taught him. For the next six decades, he continued to collect data on the making and use of bark canoes. He compiled boxes and boxes of notes and sketches, and he made models of more than a hundred canoes, illustrating differing tribal styles, differences within tribes, and differences of design purpose. A short, low-ended canoe was the kindest to portage, and the best to paddle among the overhanging branches of a small stream. A canoe with a curving, rocker bottom could turn with quick response in white water. A canoe with a narrow bow and stern and a somewhat V-sided straight bottom could hold its course across a strong lake wind. A canoe with a narrow beam moved faster than any other and was therefore the choice for war. Adney so thoroughly dedicated himself to the preservation of knowledge of the bark canoe that he was still doing research, still getting ready to write the definitive book on the subject, when, having reached the age of eighty-one, he died. Over the next dozen years or so, Howard I. Chapelle, curator of transportation at the Smithsonian Institution, went through Adney's hills of paper and ultimately wrote the book, calling it *The Bark Canoes and Skin Boats of North America*. Large in format, it has two hundred and forty-two pages containing drawings, diagrams, photographs, and a text that frequently solidifies with technical density:

When the bark has been turned up and clamped, the gores may be trimmed to allow it to be sewn with edge-to-edge seams at each slash. This is usually done after the sides are faired, by moving the battens up and down as the cuts are made, then replacing them in their original position. The gores or slashes, if overlapped, are not usually sewn at this stage of construction.

The U.S. Government Printing Office released the book in 1964, and Henri Vaillancourt first heard of it a couple of years later, when someone passing through town happened to mention it. He sent for a copy. The book enabled him, while still in his teens, to take a big step toward the perfection he was imagining when he hacked his first boat to pieces. His second completion was, in his words, "a very tolerable canoe."

He enrolled for a while in the forestry program at the University of New Hampshire, but in a sense Adney and Chapelle had already supplied him with his college, and the one in Durham interested him less than the one he could carry anywhere under his arm. So he went home to Greenville after his freshman year (1969) and began what in all likelihood will prove to be a life's career, since he appears to be interested in almost nothing else. Nothing much enters his time, his thought, or his conversation that does not have to do with the making and use of birch-bark canoes. He is unmarried and lives with his parents. He works in a small room that was his grandfather's shop—nine by fourteen feet—in a tarpapered shed that stands separate from the house. The shed is old, and light comes in at places other than the windows, but he has an iron stove with a chimney pipe that bends shy of the ceiling and makes a long horizontal trip through the room before penetrating to the outside. This rig is more than equal to the New Hampshire winter, and Vaillancourt, eight to twelve hours a day, sits below the long chimney in his shirtsleeves, feeding the stove, and stringing snowshoes or carving paddles or shaping the ribs, thwarts, and stempieces of the next summer's canoes. A picture on a wall shows hunters in a birch-bark canoe on Long Lake in the Adirondacks in 1880. Another is a Frederic Remington print of Chippewas in a canoe with high-swept ends, riding a big tail wind on the lakelike St. Lawrence. Stored on racks are long strips of split cedar, brought from Maine, which by spring will be resplit and split again to appropriate size, then tapered and finished with the crooked knife until they are ready to be lashed together as the gunwales of a started canoe. Vaillancourt, whittling, or rough-shaping wood with an axe, sits on a rocking chair over which is draped the hide of a deer. New paddles stand against the walls, and some are inlaid with deer bone, which looks like mother-of-pearl and is set in designs of eastern Canadian tribes. He bends hickory for his snowshoes, and he strings them—in a painstaking fineness of pattern—with rawhide that he scrapes and cuts. He is not a hunter, but there is no lack of hunters in Greenville, and they give him the skins he needs. He never uses power tools. He uses a froe, an axe, an awl, a crooked knife—and with the last three alone could build a canoe. The crooked knife is the finishing instrument, the tool whose ten thousand touches yield the artistry he seeks. One does not drive to a shopping center in search of a crooked knife. Tacked to the inside of the shed door is the address where Vaillancourt sends for his: Hudson's Bay Co., Pointe Claire, P.Q.

When the weather warms and the thaw is gone, Vaillancourt comes out of the shop and works in the yard. He has built a canvas-covered lean-to against a wall of the house, and under the lean-to he starts the canoes. After some weeks, he may have as many as four under construction, each in a different stage of the process. Music falls on him from a second-story window. He keeps his stereo up there, playing country-and-Western and Beethoven symphonies. Sometimes he becomes so absorbed in the music he makes mistakes on the canoes. He can build seven a year. Most are around sixteen feet long, and for that size he charges eight hundred and fifty dollars. Even after they are gone, he remains ferociously proprietary about them. He has made them for customers as far away as Idaho, but he seems to regard each canoe as his own forever, and his profoundest hope is that it will survive its owner and then be passed on to a museum. When he can, in his travels, he visits his canoes. This satisfies his longing to know how they are doing. He is pleased also to get one "back in the yard," so he can touch it up, repair it, perhaps even improve it in the light of his continually rising skills. He refers to "the yard" as someone else might refer to the Newport News Shipbuilding & Dry Dock Company.

"The yard" is on the edge of town. A state road runs close by, and a blinking light hangs overhead: the intersection of New Hampshire 31 and Mill Street, Greenville—population sixteen hundred, a mill town sitting on hillsides, divided by a stream. Since the mills folded, smaller businesses have been set up within their walls: plastics, apples, herbs. Three of Vaillancourt's grandparents came from farms along the south bank of the St. Lawrence, in the Eastern Townships of Quebec. They came south for the money to be made in the mills, as did so many others, and not much about Greenville is English except its name. Stones in the cemetery say Rousseau, Blanchette, Bergeron, Fournier, Souliers, Chuinard, Bourgeois, Charrois, Desrosiers, McMillan, Beausoleil, Robichaud, Charbonneau, Baillargeon, Caron, Martin, Vaillancourt. French, as Henri grew up, was the language of the table at home, the language—although fading now—of the street. When Henri started school, French was used there. The change to English came soon after. Henri's mother and father (who works in a yarn mill in another town) refer to the people in surrounding towns, counties, and the rest of the United States as "*les Américains.*" Henri's name, in French, is said the way it looks. In English, he is "Henry Vallenkort" to everyone in town.

A number of completely finished canoes might be strewn around the yard at any one time, for Vaillancourt is slow to ship them out, or if people are coming to get them he is in no hurry to notify them that the canoes are ready. He likes to keep his canoes awhile—use them some, test them out. Whatever the excuse may be, he does not like to let them go. Two were there when I first saw the yard. Their bark, smooth and taut, was of differing shades of brown, trellised with dark seams. I guess I had expected something a little rough, rippled, crude, asymmetrical. These things, to the eye, were perfect in their symmetry. Their color was pleasing. Turn them over— their ribs, thwarts, and planking suggested cabinetwork. Their authenticity seemed built in, sewed in, lashed in, undeniable. In the sunlight of that cold November morning, they were the two most beautiful canoes I had ever seen. All this—when what I had frankly feared encountering were outsize, erratic souvenirs.

I had spent a good part of my early summers in canoes and on canoe trips, and all the canoes I used in those years were made of wood and canvas. They were Old Towns and E. M. Whites—lake canoes, river canoes, keeled, and keel-less. The bark canoe was gone, but not as long gone as I then—in the nineteen-thirties and forties—imagined. Now, in the nineteen-seventies, wood-and-canvas canoes were gradually becoming extinct, or seemed to be. They were seen about as frequently on canoe trails as bark canoes apparently were fifty years ago. What had replaced the wood and canvas were new generations of aluminum, Fiberglas, and plastic—canoe simulacra that lacked resonance, moved without elegance, fairly lurched through the forest. Some of them—white streaked with black —were designed to suggest birch bark. The sport in white water—where runs are made against a stopwatch—had been taken over by small Fiberglas boats that were called canoes but looked like kayaks. And now here was Henri Vaillancourt, whom I had heard of through a note in a newsletter of the Canoe Cruisers Association, standing in his yard beside bark-covered canoes—in full-time resolve to preserve them in the world—shyly and with what I then took to be modesty answering a most obvious question. Oh, don't worry, they were quite strong, really strong. They could take quite a blow. The ribs and planking were flexible, the bark elastic and durable. All

The Survival of the Bark Canoe

the wood in them had been split, none of it sawn. Split wood had more flexibility and more strength. If you hit a rock with sawn wood in your canoe you were more likely to crack the ribs and the planking. He cocked his arm and drove his fist into the bottom of one of the canoes with a punch that could have damaged a prizefighter. He is six feet tall and weighs a hundred and seventy-five pounds. The bottom of the canoe was unaffected. He remarked that the bark of the white birch was amazing stuff—strong, resinous, and waterproof. He said there was, in fact, virtually nothing the Indian canoe-makers did that was not as good as or better than what could be done with modern tools and materials.

His shyness was in his eyes—looking away, almost always, from the direction in which his voice was travelling—but not in his speech. He talked volubly, with nasal, staccato inflections, and if the subject was bark canoes he seemed in no hurry to stop. I stayed around the yard for a couple of days, and before I left we took one of the canoes and—as Vaillancourt likes to put it—"went for a spin" on a local pond. After paddling half a mile or so over rustling lily pads and open water, we rounded a point at one end of an island and Vaillancourt warned that the pond was shallow there and we might hit a rock. Crunch. We hit one. The canoe glanced off. It was moving fast—slicing, planing the water with much momentum and glide. Crunch. "Look out! There could be more!" Crunch.

The canoe moved on—dry, sound in the ribs. When we landed, we turned it over. On the bark, a couple of marks were visible of the sort that a fingernail might make on a piece of hide. "We hit a stump head on once, in Maine," he said. "And the stump, you know, split in two." He was happy enough, though, to have people go on thinking—as people apparently did—that bark canoes were fragile. Any canoe could be damaged, and the general welfare of bark canoes might be helped by this common misconception. Bark canoes were actually so strong and flexible that Indians had used them not only in heavy rapids but also on the ocean. "But they're so rare today, you know, I wouldn't sell them to people who do white water. It's not the canoes I don't trust. I fully trust the canoes to go down white water. I don't trust the people who are paddling them. Bark canoes are so rare. There's no sense in wrecking even one."

In the middle of one morning, Vaillancourt left the shop, got into his car, drove two or three miles down the road, and went into woods to cut a birch. The weather was sharp, and he was wearing a heavy red Hudson's Bay coat. His sandy-brown hair, curling out in back, rested on the collar. He carried a sheathed Hudson's Bay axe and a long wooden wedge and a wooden club (he called it a mallet) of the type seen in cartoons about cave societies. His eyes—they were pale blue, around an aquiline nose over a trapper's mustache—searched the woodlot for a proper tree. It need not be a giant. There were no giants around Greenville anyway. He wanted it for its sapwood, not its bark—for thwarts (also called crosspieces and crossbars) in a future canoe. After walking several hundred feet in from the road, he found a birch about eight inches in diameter, and with the axe he notched it in the direction of a free fall. He removed his coat and carefully set it aside. Beneath it was a blue oxford-cloth button-down shirt, tucked into his blue-jeans. He chopped the tree, and it fell into a young beech. "Jesus Christ!" he said. "It is so frustrating when Nature has you beat." The birch was hung up in the beech. He heaved at it and hauled it until it at last came free.

What he wanted of the tree was about six feet of its trunk, which he cut away from the rest. Then he sank the axe into one end of the piece, removed the axe, placed the wedge in the cut, and tapped the wedge with the mallet. He tapped twice more, and the entire log fell apart in two even halves. He said, "You get some birch, it's a bastard to split out, I'll tell you. But, Christ, this is nice. That's good and straight grain. Very often you get them twisted." Satisfied, he shouldered the tools and the wood, went back to the road, and drove home.

In the yard, he split the birch again, and he now had four pieces, quarter-round. One of these he cut off to a length of about forty inches. He took that into the shed. He built a fire, and in minutes the room was warm. He sat in his rocking chair and addressed the axe to the quarter-round log—the dark heartwood, the white sapwood. Holding the piece vertically, one end resting on the floor, he cut the heartwood away. He re-moved the bark and then went rapidly down the sapwood making angled indentations that caused the wood to curve out like petals. He cut them off, and they fell as big chips to the floor. A pile began to grow there as the axe head moved up and down, and what had been by appearance firewood was in a short time converted to lumber—a two-by-three, knotless board that might almost have been sawn in a mill.

He then picked up his crooked knife and held its grip in his upturned right hand, the blade poking out to the left. The blade was bent near its outer end (enabling it to move in grooves and hollows where the straight part could not). Both blade and grip were shaped like nothing I had ever seen. The grip, fashioned for the convenience of a hand closing over it, was bulbous. The blade had no hinge and protruded rigidly —but not straight out. It formed a shallow V with the grip.

Vaillancourt held the piece of birch like a violin, sighting along it from his shoulder, and began to carve, bringing the knife upward, toward his chest. Of all the pieces of a canoe, the center thwart is the most complicated in the carving. Looked at from above, it should be broad at the midway point, then taper gradually as it reaches toward the sides of the canoe. Near its ends, it flares out in shoulders that are penetrated by holes, for lashings that will help secure it to the gunwales. The long taper, moreover, is interrupted by two grooved protrusions, where a tumpline can be tied before a portage. The whole upper surface should be flat, but the underside of the thwart rises slightly from the middle outward, then drops again at the ends, the result being that the thwart is thickest in the middle, gradually thinning as it extends outward and thickening again at the gunwales. All of this comes, in the end, to an adroit ratio between strength and weight, not to mention the incidental grace of the thing, each of its features being a mirror image of another. The canoe's central structural element, it is among the first parts set in place. Its long dimension establishes the canoe's width, and therefore many of the essentials of the canoe's design. In portage, nearly all of the weight of the canoe bears upon it.

So to me the making of a center thwart seemed a job for a jigsaw, a band saw, a set of chisels, a hammer, a block plane, a grooving plane, calipers, templates, and—most of all—mechanical drawings. One would have thought that anyone assertive enough to try it with a knife alone would at least begin slowly, moving into the wood with caution. Vaillancourt, to the contrary, tore his way in. He brought the knife toward him with such strong, fast, heavy strokes that long splinters flew off the board. "Birch is good stuff to work with," he said. "It's almost as easy to work as cedar. This feels like a hot knife going through butter. I used to use a drawknife. That God-damned thing. You've got to use a vise to hold the work. With the crooked knife, I can work in the woods if I want. I saw an Indian on TV in Canada using one. I got one, and I worked and worked with it to get the knack. Now it almost feels as if it's part of me. If anybody ever comes out with a tool that will rival a crooked knife, I'd like to hear about it." He sighted along the wood, turned it over, and began whipping splinters off the other side. He said that steel tools had come with the white man, of course, and that most people seemed to imagine that Indian workmanship had improved with steel tools. "But I doubt it," he continued. "With bone and stone tools, it just took longer. The early Indians relied more on abrasion. With the exception of the center thwart, there is no fancy carving in a canoe. It's all flatwork. In fact, I'm doing experiments with bone tools." He stopped carving, reached to a shelf, and picked up a bone awl. "Make two holes with a bone awl in a piece of cedar, take out the wood between the holes with a bone chisel, and you have a mortise for a thwart to fit into." He reached for a piece of cedar (wood debris was all over the shop), made two holes, picked up a wooden mallet and a bone chisel, and made a mortise in the cedar. Then he picked up the long, curving incisor of a beaver. "I made a knife last winter out of a beaver's tooth," he said. "The original crooked knife was made out of a beaver's tooth." He sat down and continued to carve. The strokes were lighter now as he studied the wood, carved a bit, studied the wood, and carved some more. The piece was beginning to look roughly like a thwart, and the gentler motions of the knife were yielding thin, curling shavings that settled down on the bed of chips and splinters around his feet.

"Where the crooked knife was, the bark canoe was," he said. "People from Maine recognize the crooked knife. People from New Hampshire do not. All they knew was the drawknife. The God-damned drawknife—what a bummer."

The bark canoe was also where the big white birches were, and that excluded a good part of New Hampshire, including

The Survival of the Bark Canoe

Greenville. Vaillancourt goes north to find his bark. The range of the tree—*Betula papyrifera,* variously called the white birch, the silver birch, the paper birch, the canoe birch—forms a swath more than a thousand miles wide (more or less from New York City to Hudson Bay) and reaches westward and northwestward to the Pacific. Far in from the boundaries of this enormous area, though, the trees are unlikely and always have been unlikely to grow large enough for the building of good canoes, and this exclusion includes most of the West, and even the Middle West. The biggest trees and the best of Indian canoes were in what are now New Brunswick, Nova Scotia, Maine, Quebec, and parts of Ontario. Even within this region, the most accomplished craftsmen were concentrated in the east. Of these, the best were the Malecites. So Henri Vaillancourt builds Malecite canoes. Before all other design factors, he cares most about the artistic appearance of the canoes he builds, and he thinks the best-looking were the canoes of the Malecites. The Malecites lived in New Brunswick and parts of Maine. Vaillancourt builds the Malecite St. John River Canoe and the Malecite St. Lawrence River Canoe. He builds them with modifications, though. Toward the end of the nineteenth century, tribes started copying one another and gave up some of the distinctiveness of their tribal styles, and to varying extents, he said, he has done the same.

His carving became even slower now, and he studied the piece carefully before making his moves, but he measured nothing. "There's really no need for feet and inches," he said. "I know more or less what's strong and what isn't. If I want to find the middle of this crosspiece, I can put a piece of bark across it from end to end, and then fold it in half to find the center." He had measured the length—thirty-five inches—and had cut to it exactly. In the spring, when the time came to make the gunwales, he would measure them as well. But that is all he would measure in the entire canoe. According to the prescript passed on by Adney and Chapelle, the center thwart he was working on should taper

slightly in thickness each way from its center to within 5 inches of the shoulders, which are 30 inches apart. The thickness at a point 5 inches from the shoulder is ¾ inch; from there the taper is quick to the shoulder, which is ⁵⁄₁₆ inch thick, with a drop to ¼ inch in the tenon. The width, 3 inches at the center, decreases in a graceful curve to within 5 inches of the shoulder, where it is 2 inches, then increases to about 3 inches at the shoulder. The width of the tenon is, of course, 2 inches, to fit the mortise hole in the gunwale.

Yet the only instruments Vaillancourt was using to meet these specifications were his eyes.

He finished off the tumpline grooves. The thwart appeared to be perfect, but he picked up a piece of broken glass and scraped it gently all over. Fine excelsior came away, and the surface became shiningly smooth. It was noon. He had cut the birch in the woods at half past nine. Now he held the thwart in his hand, turning it this way and that. It was a lovely thing in itself, I thought, for it had so many blendings of symmetry. He said he could have done it in an hour if he had not been talking so much. And he was glad the tree in the woods had turned into this thwart instead of "all the chintzy two-bit things they make out of birch—clothespins, dowels, toothpicks, Popsicle sticks." As he worked, he had from time to time scooped up handfuls of chips and shavings and fed them into the stove. Even so, the pile was still high around him, and he appeared to be sitting in a cone of snow.

He soon added more to the pile. From the rafters he took down a piece of cedar and, with the knife, sent great strips of it flying to the floor. He was now making a stempiece, the canoe part that establishes the profile of the bow or the stern.

The Survival of the Bark Canoe

"Sometimes, when there are, you know, contortions in the grain, you can get into a real rat's nest," he said. "Around a knot, there will be waves in the grain. You cut to the knot from one side, then the other, to get a straight edge. At times like that, I'm tempted just to throw the thing out."

The wood he was working now, though, was clear and without complications, and after a short while, in which most of it went to the floor, he had made something that looked very much like a yardstick—albeit a heavy one—a half inch thick. Its corners were all sharp, and it seemed to have been machine-planed. Then he pressed the blade of the crooked knife into one end of the stick and kept pressing just hard enough to split the stick down fifty per cent of its length. He pressed the knife into the end again, near the first cut, and made another split, also stopping halfway. Again and again he split the wood, going far beyond the moment when I, watching him, thought that further splitting would be impossible, would ruin the whole. He split the board thirty-one times— into laminations each a half inch wide and a sixteenth of an inch thick. And all the laminations stopped in the middle, still attached there; from there on, the wood remained solid. "You split cedar parallel to the bark," he commented. "Hickory you can split both ways. There are very few woods you can do that with."

He plunged the laminated end of the piece into a bucket of water and left it there for a while, and then he built up the fire with scraps from the floor. In a coffee can he brought water to a boil. He poured it slowly over the laminations, bathing them, bathing them again. Then he lifted the steaming cedar in two hands and bent it. The laminations slid upon one another and formed a curve. He pondered the curve. It was not enough of a curve, he decided. So he bent the piece a little more. "There's an awful lot of it that's just whim," he said. "You vary the stempiece by whim." He liked what he saw now, so he reached for a strip of basswood bark, tightly wound it around the curve in the cedar, and tied it off. The basswood bark was not temporary. It would stay there, and go into the canoe. Bow or stern, the straight and solid part of the stem-piece would run downward from the tip, then the laminated curve would sweep inward, establishing the character of the end—and thus, in large part, of the canoe itself.

The canoe-end profile was the principal feature that dis-tinguished the styles of the tribes. The Ojibway Long-Nose Canoe, for example, had in its bow (and stern) an outreach-ing curve of considerable tumblehome (an arc—like a paren-thesis—that turns more than ninety degrees and begins to come back on itself). The end profiles of the Algonquin Hunter's Canoe were straight and almost vertical, with a small-radius ninety-degree curve at the waterline. The depar-ture from the vertical was inward, toward the paddler. The end profiles of certain Malecite canoes were similar, but the departure from vertical was outward. Other Malecite canoes had long-radius, "compass sweep" bows and sterns.

I mentioned to Vaillancourt that, before and during col-lege years, I had spent a lot of time around a place in Ver-mont that still specializes in sending out canoe trips, and a birch-bark canoe hangs in the dining hall there.

"Near Salisbury," he said. "Lake Dunmore—am I right?" He took down a worn, filled notebook and began to whip the pages. "Let's see. Yeah. Here. Keewaydin. Is that it?"

That was it. He had not been there, but he would stop by someday. He hoped to see every bark canoe in existence. There were, for example, sixteen bark canoes in Haliburton, Ontario; one in Upper Canada Village, near Morrisburg, Ontario; a couple at Old Jesuit House, in Sillery, Quebec. In his note-book he had the names and addresses of museums, historical societies, and individuals from Maine to Minnesota, Nova Scotia to Alberta, and as far south as Virginia. Peter Paul, a

---

The Survival of the Bark Canoe

Malecite in Woodstock, New Brunswick, had one. Vaillancourt had been to see him. The most skillfully built birch-bark canoe he had ever seen was made in Old Town, Maine, and was signed "Louis P. Sock." "I've seen only two or three canoes that were near perfect," he said. "But I've never seen a bark canoe that wasn't graceful. I've never seen an Eastern Cree canoe or a Montagnais. Most of the canoes I've seen did not have a definite tribal style. There's a bark canoe on Prince Edward Island. A sign says it's a Micmac canoe. It isn't."

I told him I'd long ago been told that the bark canoe at Keewaydin was an Iroquois.

He said he doubted that very much, because the Iroquois, except in early times, had had limited access to good birch, and had made their canoes—when they made canoes at all—out of elm or hickory bark. Various tribes had also used the bark of the spruce, the basswood, the chestnut. But all were crude compared to birch. If they wanted to get across a river, they might—in one day—build an elm-bark canoe, and then forget it, leave it in the woods. "You couldn't, by any stretch of the imagination, compare an elm-bark or a hickory-bark canoe to a birch canoe," he said. "Barks other than birch bark will absorb water the way wood will. Canoes made from them —even well made—got waterlogged and heavy. Most were just, you know, rough shells. Good for nothing, like automobiles. Automobiles last, you know, five or six years. A birch-bark canoe lasted the Indians ten."

I asked him how much experience he had had by now in more modern canoes. He said he had been in an aluminum canoe twice and in wood-and-canvas canoes only a few times in his life. Otherwise, he had never paddled anything but a birch-bark canoe. He did not paddle much around home, he said, because when he went canoeing he wanted to go to Maine.

"Where in Maine?"

"Oh, up north of Moosehead Lake. The Penobscot River. Chesuncook Lake. Caucomgomoc Lake. It's not just to get out in the canoe—it's to get out and see wildlife. A moose, you know, thirty feet away. Next time I go, I'm going down the Penobscot and on to the Allagash lakes."

I said, "Next time you go, I'd like to go with you."

He said, "Bring your own food."

I had been yearning to make a trip into that region for what was now most of my life. Keewaydin had run trips there, but one circumstance or another had always prevented me from going. Just the thought of making a journey there in a birch-bark canoe was enough to make me sway like a drunk. I thought of little else through the winter and the spring.

It is five-fifteen in the morning, August 12th, and Henri is up splitting cedar. The lake is smooth. The far shore is indistinct in rising mist. A loon, attracted to the sound of the axe, cruises near. When the axe stops, the loon laughs. Two tents. Two canoes—resting on their sides. The firewood, which is driftwood, is so dry that the fire is almost as quiet as the sun, which is still too low to cut through the mist. The air is cold.

Henri is splitting out pieces eighteen feet long. He cut the tree green two years ago and left it in the woods here—seven miles from the roadhead—to season. Now he has begun this trip by coming to retrieve the cedar, to carry it out the seven miles across the gunwales of his canoe. The split strips, which themselves will become gunwales in months ahead, will ride more stably than would a solid log.

There are five of us. The Blanchette brothers—Rick and Mike, friends of Henri's from Greenville—are eating oatmeal for breakfast. Warren Elmer and I have tea and dried fruit. Warren and I are from the same town in New Jersey. He is a teacher of environmental studies at Washington International

School. He is a backpacker by choice and experience, and this is his first long canoe trip.

Henri, finished with his work, opens a paper bag and eats jerky. That is his breakfast. Last night, he ate jerky for dinner. The Blanchettes have their food. Warren and I have ours. Henri has his. He insists on this arrangement. He says that on one canoe trip he made he tried eating the communal way but "that was a real bummer; someone always ate all the food," and he will never do it again.

The Blanchettes' tent is small, low, nylon. It weighs three and a half pounds, and somewhat bulgingly sleeps two. They own a larger one, but Henri insisted that they leave it home, to eliminate the extra weight. The other tent is mine, sleeps three, and is a pavilion you can stand up in. Henri, when he first saw it, said not to bring it, that it was too heavy, and too bulky.

In the yard in Greenville, we had a general weed-out of equipment. The back of my car was full of stuff, and Henri looked it over. I showed him my candle-powered folding lantern.

"Forget it," he said. "You don't need it. You can get around, you know, about as well in the dark as you can in the daylight."

"How about just a candle or two?"

"They're not necessary."

I showed him my reflector baker.

"Hang it up," he said.

How about Warren's gas-powered emergency trail stove?

"Forget it."

My white-water paddle?

"If we need a spare, I can make one."

My fishing rod?

"Forget it. Who wants to carry, you know, all that junk on a portage?"

The Survival of the Bark Canoe

I showed him the tent. Rolled up, it was a cylinder eight inches in diameter and four feet long. It weighed eighteen pounds.

"Hang it up," he said. "The idea is to travel light."

How much equipment goes on a canoe trip is a reflection of the criteria that go along as well. Young Indians of the Maine woods, several centuries ago, went off alone for upward of a year—to prove their skills and their ability to survive. They took a canoe, a spear, some bone tools, a crooked knife, snowshoes, and a blanket. Today, if someone's criterion is to play at being an Indian, that is how to do it. Henri knew too much about the Indians to pretend to be one. He was a craftsman— an artist, really—with a historical purpose, not a boy with a feather in his hair. His professed criteria were to take it easy, see some wildlife, and travel light with his bark canoes— nothing more—and one could not help but lean his way. I had known of people who took collapsible cots, down pillows, chain saws, outboard motors, cases of beer, and battery-powered portable refrigerators on canoe trips—even into deep wilderness. You set your own standards. Travel by canoe is not a necessity, and will nevermore be the most efficient way to get from one region to another, or even from one lake to another—anywhere. A canoe trip has become simply a rite of oneness with certain terrain, a diversion of the field, an act performed not because it is necessary but because there is value in the act itself; and what you take along depends on what you can afford (Henri could not afford to buy beef jerky, so he had to make it) and on how you see yourself in the setting.

Indians slept in pairs under their canoes—feet touching in the center, heads toward the ends. Henri had tried sleeping under a canoe once, too, but would never try it again. Ultimately, he changed his mind and decided that it would be a good idea to take my tent after all, because he could fit into it with Warren and me. I needed the reflector baker. Much of the food I had brought depended on its use. So I stowed it where he wouldn't see it. Deep in my pack basket I had a small flashlight. I decided not to tell Henri it was there.

I unrolled a set of topographic maps I had bought, and asked him to show us our route. He said he had no idea what the route would be and didn't care to think about it. We would leave a car at each of two roadheads—one at North East Carry, the other at Caucomgomoc Lake—but the trip we made between these two points would not be direct and would not be pressured by a plan. There would be no big rush. There was no point in rushing. Travel light. Take it easy. See the wildlife. I rolled up the maps.

Rick Blanchette was bringing his own canoe—one of the early ones that Vaillancourt had made. Henri, for himself, had selected a small one from the inventory then in the yard. It was narrow of beam, nine inches deep, and only thirteen and a half feet long. It was particularly attractive—covered almost wholly with a single sheet of bark—and it was light to carry. Rick Blanchette was worried, though, that the canoe was too small to bear two men and their gear, so Henri took it to the pond to try it out. With a single paddler in it, and no gear, it was a poised and responsive canoe, but with three of us in it —aggregating five hundred pounds—it showed too much instability and very nearly ate the pond. Henri decided to leave it home. He chose a longer canoe instead—a canoe he had made for Idaho State University and would crate for shipment in a moon or two. He put it on sawhorses, right side up, and poured into it a couple of buckets of water. Almost none dripped through.

Our packs, in final form, pleased Henri, and he said so. The Blanchettes each had a pack frame. Warren and I each had a pack basket. Henri stuffed his personal food and gear

The Survival of the Bark Canoe

into two pack baskets, tied the canoes to my car and his, and in early morning we started north. He led the way, and we drove ten hours without stopping for food.

Between Rockwood, Maine (about halfway up Moosehead Lake), and Allagash, Maine (at the confluence of the Allagash and St. John Rivers), there is an area of about five thousand square miles in which is neither a paved nor a public road. What few roads there are "north of the Moosehead" have dirt-and-gravel surfaces and are travelled by the public, at the public's risk, courtesy of the paper companies that own the land. We drove the last hour into the woods on these roads, and put the canoes into the West Branch of the Penobscot River at six in the evening. The current was strong but unbroken, flowing between walls of spruce. Swiftly moving, loaded, the canoes looked superb—their duffel, compactly secured, implying days and distances of travel, implying less an excursion than a *modus vivendi*. Henri and Warren were one crew, the Blanchettes and I the other. Warren, as he paddled, looked Norse, his billowing beard projecting downriver under a tumult of blond hair. Our canoe, all things included, had between six and seven hundred pounds in it. Rick Blanchette—slight, not particularly tall, dark hair, a modest mustache—looked weightless, but his brother, well over six feet and athletically built, seemed to make up the difference. The total poundage in Henri's canoe was around four hundred and fifty. It was the shorter of the two—about fifteen and a half feet—and it had a low freeboard. In the center, three inches separated the top of the gunwale from the surface of the river. The canoe's interior depth was only ten and a half inches. It glided, though, with momentum and balance. Our canoe was nearly a foot deep, from center thwart to ribs, and it was sixteen feet long. It bore its heavier load with a higher freeboard and moved well under the paddles. Each paddle was decorated with incised line pictures of moose or with various Indian vine-and-leaf designs, and each was signed on its grip "H.A.V."—Henri Armand Vaillancourt.

Each canoe had a fleur-de-lis on its stern, and Blanchette's had as well a complex abstract design done in porcupine quills. After French priests converted the Malecites, fish designs began appearing on Malecite canoes that were launched on Fridays. On some Malecite canoes, a lynx would be drawn on one side and on the other a rabbit smoking a pipe. The rabbit symbolized the tribe. The lynx was the rabbit's mortal enemy. That the rabbit could calmly smoke a pipe so near the lynx showed the cool of the Malecite in the presence of enemies. These pictures were generally created by scraping away rind from the bark. And that is how Vaillancourt had made the fleurs-de-lis on his canoe. The bark of a birch-bark canoe is always inside out. The side that touched the wood of the tree is the side that touches the river. Rind clings only to bark that is taken in winter. There was a practical function in the designs the Indians scraped into it. The designs were a way to indicate the bow or the stern. Birch-bark canoes are not —like their progeny—reversible, because where one piece of bark is sewn to another there is a slight overlap, and the overlap faces the stern, so the seams will not be torn open when the canoe scrapes over a rock.

The evening was cool, and there was much laughing and joking as we moved along. After half an hour, we checked the canoes for leaks. They were all but completely dry.

"I have a small leak in back here," Rick said.

"*C'est dommage*," said Henri.

We turned into a small tributary. The lake where Henri had hidden the cedar was less than two miles upstream.

The sky after dark was as clear as a lens. There was no moon. We stood on the shore, tilted back our heads, looked up past the branches of the jack pines, and watched for shooting stars. One after another they came, at intervals too short to require patience. All the stars in the canopy seemed closer. We were so far out into the clear. There is more to Maine than exists in the imagination. Henri's house in New Hampshire is a lot closer to New York City than it is to this lakeshore in Maine. Maine is half of New England. It is as large as New Hampshire, Vermont, Connecticut, Rhode Island, and Massachusetts put together. And most of Maine is in the north woods, reaching embarrassingly far into Canada. Our trip would move in a northerly direction, and we had scarcely begun it, yet the lake we were camped by was a good bit north of Montreal. A shooting star burst with almost frightening brightness, illuminating our faces, lighting the sky like a flare. A loon wailed, long and mournfully. We stayed up late—to ten-thirty—too pleased with Maine to go to sleep.

We had hoped to see a moose even by now, but none has yet appeared in lake, stream, or river. Meanwhile, the loon will do. He is out there cruising still, in the spiralling morning mist, looking for fish, trolling. He trolls with his eyes. Water streams across his forehead as he moves along, and he holds his eyes just below the surface, watching the interior of the lake. He is gone. He saw something, and he is no doubt eating it now. When he dives, he just disappears. As a diver, there is nothing like him. Not even mergansers can dive like the loon. His wings close tight around his body, condensing everything —feathers, flesh—and he goes down like a powered stone, his big feet driving. He is known as the great northern diver. He can go two hundred feet down. He can swim faster than most fish. What he catches he eats without delay. His bill is always empty when he returns to the surface, and fifteen fish might be in his stomach. Because loons eat trout and young salmon, sportsmen (so-called) have been wont to shoot them— a mistaken act in any respect, because loons eat as well the natural enemies (suckers, for example) of salmon and trout.

He is up again now, not far from where he disappeared. When a loon dives, you never know where to look for him next. In what seems no time, he may break the surface far down the lake, or he may come up where he made his dive. This one is not about to go far. He is too interested in us. He cruises now with only his head and neck above the water—his conning tower. If something scares him, he can swim with only his beak out, a straw in the air—invisible if there's a ripple on the lake. Now his body is up again, and he laughs. If the laugh were human, it would be a laugh of the deeply insane. The bird's lower jaw opens and claps shut five times in each laugh. If, from where you watch, he is swimming in silhouette, you can count the movements of the jaw. He can laugh two or three ways, and he can also squeal like a puppy. But it is with another sound—a long cry in the still of the night—that the loon authenticates the northern lake. The cry is made with the neck stretched forward, and it is a sound that seems to have come up a tube from an unimaginably deep source—hardly from a floating bird. It is a high, resonant, single unvaried tone that fades at the end toward a lower register. It has caused panic, because it has been mistaken for the cry of a wolf, but it is far too ghostly for that. It is detached from the earth. The Crees believed that it was the cry of a dead warrior forbidden entry to Heaven. The Chipewyans heard it as an augury of death. Whatever it may portend, it is the predominant sound in this country. Every time the loon cry comes, it sketches its own surroundings—a remote lake under stars so bright they whiten clouds, a horizon jagged with spruce.

The loon here is laughing again, so I laugh back. He laughs. I laugh. He laughs. I laugh. He will keep it up until I am hoarse. He likes conversation. He talks this way with other loons. I am endeavoring to tell him that he is a hopeless degenerate killer of trout. He laughs.

The Survival of the Bark Canoe

His flesh is tough. The Indians boiled him until he fell apart in shreds. He looks like a big duck, a small goose. His back, in summer, is a tessellation of white squares and dots on a black field. His head is black and forest green, and so is his neck, which is surrounded with vertical white stripes. His eyes are red. In the air, he could be part flamingo—long neck extended, feet behind, back humped. His maximum airspeed is sixty miles an hour, and his stall-out speed must be fifty-nine. Anyway, he scarcely slows up, apparently because he thinks he will fall. He lands on his stomach (not feet first, like a duck), and at sixty miles an hour his landing is something to see. Ashore, he flops helplessly, vulnerably. His nest is a foot or two from water. Takeoff is a considerable problem for him. With, say, ten fish in him, he needs a runway at least a quarter of a mile long. He runs over the surface of the lake on his big feet and beats the water with his wings. Heavily, he goes into the air. With fifteen fish in him, he has no chance whatsoever. For takeoff, he needs, as well, a breeze to head into—sometimes a pretty stiff one. From a calm lake—even if he has an empty stomach—he cannot fly.

He sleeps on the water. St. Nicholas magazine, in 1910, told a story of a man—a white man, a summer camper—who in early morning paddled across a northern lake, silently approached a sleeping loon, and captured it with his hands. The article was illustrated, and showed the man reaching for the loon—from a bark canoe.

The days are hot, and we often dip our cups in the river. Henri prefers Tang. He has the powder in his pack and a plastic jug by his feet as he paddles. He also has a supply of white bread— several loaves of it—and when he is hungry he pours honey onto the bread. In five minutes, he can prepare and finish a meal. Then he is ready to move on. We are in no hurry, like the shooting stars.

The river has many riffles, too minor to be labelled rapids. Nonetheless, they are stuffed with rock. The angle of the light is not always favorable. The rocks are hidden, and—smash— full tilt we hit them. The rocks make indentations that move along the bottom of the canoe, pressing in several inches and tracing a path toward the stern. It is as if the canoe were a pliant film sliding over the boulders. Still, I feel sorry and guilty when we hit one. I have been in white water and Rick has not, so he has asked me to paddle in the stern—to steer, to pick the route, to read the river—and I reward his confidence by smashing into another rock. Nothing cracks. If this were an aluminum canoe, it would be dented now, and, I must con-

The Survival of the Bark Canoe

fess, I would not really care. Of all the differences between this canoe and others I have travelled in, the first difference is a matter of care about them. The canoes can take a lot more abuse than we give them, but we all care. Landing, we are out of the canoes and in the water ourselves long before the bark can touch bottom. We load and launch in a foot of water. The Indians did just that, and the inclination to copy them is automatic—is not consciously remembered—with these Indian canoes.

Once, on the upper Delaware, in a fifteen-foot rented Grumman canoe, I ran through a pitch of white water called Skinner's Falls. On a big shelf of rock at the bottom of the rapid, a crowd of people watched. When the canoe came through dry, they gathered around and asked how that was done. They said they were novices—a ski club on a summer outing—and none of them had been able to run the rapid without taking in quantities of water. "Well," said my wife, getting out of our canoe, "if you think you've seen anything yet, just wait until you see what is going to happen now. My husband spent his whole childhood doing this sort of thing—and so did that man up there in the other canoe. The two of them are now going to run the rapid together."

I walked up the riverbank. When I joined my friend and got into his canoe (also a fifteen-foot aluminum), I saw that one of the skiers had set up a tripod on which was mounted a sixteen-millimetre movie camera. My wife later told me she had said to them that it was good that they had the camera, because they would be able to study the film and learn a great deal. Skinner's Falls is easiest on the right. It gets worse and worse the farther to the left you go. So, for the rash hell of it, we dug in hard, got up to high speed, and went into the extreme left side of the rapid. The canoe bucked twice before the bow caught a rock that swung us broadside to the current and into a protruding boulder with a crash that threw us into the white river and bent the canoe into the shape of the letter C.

I have chosen not to tell that story to Rick Blanchette, for no one has ever cared more for a fifteen-thousand-dollar sports car (or, for that matter, for a work of sculpture) than he cares for his birch canoe.

Henri hits a rock; slides right; hits another. "I'd venture to say it would be easier to rip a wood-and-canvas canoe than a birchbark," he says. "Anyhow, I've never, you know, ripped one." Henri paddles like an Indian. His stroke is a short, light, rapid chop. White people tend to take longer, harder strokes, which use a great deal more energy, he says. He appears relaxed in the stern of his canoe—leaning back, looking for wild-life, his paddle in motion like a wire whisk. Warren, in the bow, digs a large hole in the river with every stroke, contributing to the over-all effort the higher part of the ratio of power. We kneel, of course, and lean against the thwarts. There are no seats in these canoes. Kneeling is the natural paddling position anyway. It lowers the center of gravity, adds to the canoe's stability, brings more of the body into the stroke. Arms don't ache. You don't get tired.

We are seeing only ducks and muskrats on the big river, so we go into small streams in search of moose. These tributaries, tortuous and boggy, have all the appearance of moose country —Pine Stream, Moosehorn Stream. Moose tracks are everywhere—great cloven depressions in the mudbanks. Paddling silently, we move upstream—half, three-quarters of a mile. No moose. Henri is good at the silent paddle—the blade feathered on the recovery from each stroke and never coming out of the water. However, he is having difficulty travelling in the channel. The stream is only a few yards wide and has many bends. The canoes keep hitting the banks and sticking in the mud. With some trepidation, I suggest that there are bow

The Survival of the Bark Canoe

strokes—draw, cross-draw, draw-stroke, pry, cross-pry—intended to help the canoe avoid the banks of the river. Trepidation because it is astonishing how people sometimes resent being told how to paddle a canoe. I have paddled on narrow, twisting rivers in New Jersey with good friends—easygoing, even-tempered people—who got royally incensed when I suggested that if they would only learn to draw and cross-draw they would not continue to plow the riverbanks. The look in their eyes showed a sense of insult, resting on the implication that every human being is born knowing how to use a canoe. The canoe itself apparently inspires such attitudes, because in form it is the most beautifully simple of all vehicles. And the born paddlers keep hitting the banks of the rivers. Mike Blanchette, though, in the bow of our canoe, to my relief, is not offended. Nor is Warren. They quickly pick up the knack of the pry and the draw—ways of moving the bow suddenly to left or right. Henri shows interest, too, inadvertently revealing that he knows almost nothing about paddling in the bow. His interest is genuine but academic. The bow is the subordinate position in a canoe. The person in the stern sets the course, is the pilot, the captain. The Blanchettes and I regularly change positions in our canoe, but Henri never leaves the stern.

Eventually, we give up the mooselook and go back to the main stream. Henri says it is all but impossible to go down the West Branch of the Penobscot River from North East Carry to Chesuncook Lake without seeing a number of—not to mention one—moose. Deriding us, a screaming seagull flies high above the river. We are two hundred river miles from the sea. Some substitute. In lieu of a moose, a seagull.

The Abnakis lived here. And the first whites to come into this lake-and-river country were hunters. They went back with stories of white pines so big that four men, grasping hands, could not reach around them. The next whites who came were timber cruisers. They made trips not unlike the one we are making—wandering at will in bark canoes—noting, and marking on inexact maps, the stands of pine. The big trees were there for the taking. They tended to cluster on the shores of the lakes. Loggers and log drivers followed, of course. Indian, hunter, cruiser, lumberer—this progression, in such beautiful country, could not help but lead to the tourist, the canoe-tripping tourist, and among the first of these (in all likelihood, *the* first tourist in the Maine woods) was Henry David Thoreau. He made two bark-canoe trips here, in 1853 and 1857, each time with an Indian guide. He went down this river. He went to the lake where Henri Vaillancourt—a hundred and twenty years later—would hide the felled cedar. Looking for moose in the night, he went up Moosehorn Stream. No moose. He had in his pack some pencils and an oilskin pouch full of scratch paper—actually letters that customers had written to his family's business, ordering plumbago and other printing supplies. On the backs of these discarded letters he made condensed, fragmentary, scarcely legible notes, and weeks later, when he had returned home to Concord, he composed his journal of the trip, slyly using the diary form, and writing at times in the present tense, to gain immediacy, to create the illusion of paragraphs written—as it is generally supposed they were written—virtually in the moments described. With the advantage of retrospect, he reconstructed the story to reveal a kind of significance that the notes do not reveal. Something new in journalism. With the journal as his principal source, he later crafted still another manuscript, in which he further shaped and rearranged the story, all the while adhering to a structure built on calendar dates. The result, published posthumously in hardcover form, was the book he called *The Maine Woods*.

Henri Vaillancourt's familiarity with books appears to be narrow, but he has read Thoreau—from *Walden* to *Cape Cod*, and most notably *The Maine Woods*. Rick Blanchette is saturated in Thoreau. In every segment of the river, they remember things Thoreau did there—places where he camped, where he collected flora, where he searched for moose. "I'm into Thoreau, too," Mike has said. "He writes about pickerel fishing, turtle hunting—the things I know and do."

Vaillancourt is transfixed by the knowledge that Thoreau, at North East Carry, actually watched a group of Indians making bark canoes. "All of them sitting there whittling with crooked knives! What a life! I'd give anything to have been there."

Back and forth between our two canoes, bits of Thoreau fly all day.

"Thoreau said the nose of the moose was the greatest delicacy, and after that the tongue."

"Thoreau said it is a common accident for men camping in the woods to be killed by a falling tree."

"Do you remember during the Allagash and East Branch trip when he said that all heroes and discoverers were insane?"

"No, that was in *Cape Cod*."

"Some people think he was humorless, you know. I disagree."

"Thoreau said . . ."

"Thoreau believed . . ."

"Do you remember the passage where . . ."

When it is not my turn to paddle and I am riding in the center of the canoe, I read to catch up. Thoreau's trips were provisioned with smoked beef, coffee, sugar, tea, plum cake, salt, pepper, and lemons for flavoring the water. His tent was made from cut poles and cotton cloth. He had one blanket. He carried his gear in India-rubber bags, and it included an extra shirt, extra socks, two waistcoats, six dickies, a thick nightcap, a four-quart tin pail, a jackknife, a fishline, hooks, pins, needles, thread, matches, an umbrella, a towel, and soap. For foul weather, he had an India-rubber coat, in which he sweated uncomfortably and got wetter than he would have in the rain. He ate his meals from birch-bark plates, using forks whittled from alder. For relief from mosquitoes, he wore a veil; he also threw damp leaves onto the fire and sat in the smoke. He slept in smoke, too—burning wet rotting logs all night.

Thoreau's guide on the first canoe trip was Joe Aitteon, and, on the second, Joe Polis—both Penobscots from Indian Island in Old Town, Maine. Henri Vaillancourt is at least as interested in these Indians as he is in Thoreau—particularly in Polis, who made his own canoes. Polis and Aitteon travelled light—no changes of clothing. Aitteon was a log driver. Polis was the better woodsman. Polis had represented his tribe in Washington. He had visited New York. He said, "I suppose, I live in New York, I be poorest hunter, I expect." Thoreau hired him for eleven dollars a week, which included the use of his canoe. Some eighteen feet in length, thirty inches wide, and a foot deep in the center, it was a longer, narrower canoe than the Vaillancourt canoes we are using. Thoreau's first canoe—on the 1853 trip with Aitteon—was more than nineteen feet long, and the bark was painted green. Our paddles are made from birch. Thoreau's were made from sugar maple. Thoreau was discomforted by the confinement of the paddling position, and he used the word "torture" to describe it. Sometimes he stood up in the canoe to stretch his legs. He appreciated nonetheless the genius of canoe technology. "The canoe implies a long antiquity in which its manufacture has been gradually perfected," he wrote in his journal. "It will ere long, perhaps, be ranked among the lost arts."

When Thoreau, from Mt. Katahdin, saw neither clearings nor cabins across huge domains of forest, lake, and river, he said, "It did not look as if a solitary traveller had cut so much as a walking-stick there." On closer view, though, from water level, he saw the stumps of timber a great deal larger than walking sticks. He saw dry-ki, too. The first dams (small dams, built to raise the lakes a few feet to serve, in various ways, the convenience of logging companies) had been built in 1841, and now, after a dozen years and more, "great trunks of trees stood dead and bare far out in the lake, making the impression of ruined piers of a city that had been—while behind, the timber lay criss-a-cross for half a dozen rods or more over the water." Dry-ki (the syllables rhyme) apparently derives from "dry kill": wood killed as a result of the dams and now, as dry as bone—gray, resins gone—crudely fencing the shores of open water. Thoreau always hoped to see some caribou but saw none. Of the caribou, Polis said, "No likum stump. When he sees that he scared."

The stumps that scared Thoreau were the stumps of the giant pines. To cut and take those trees was "as if individual speculators were to be allowed to export the clouds out of the sky, or the stars out of the firmament, one by one." If the attitudes behind such rapine were to go on unchecked, he said (a century and a quarter before the great ecological uprising), "we shall be reduced to gnaw the very crust of the earth for nutriment." And what of the remaining "stately pines"? Twenty years before the first national park, and more than a century before the Wilderness Act, he asked, "Why should not we . . . have our national preserves, where . . . the bear and panther . . . may still exist, and not be 'civilized off the face of the earth'?" The Maine of his bark-canoe trips was the deepest wilderness Thoreau would see in his lifetime. Today, astonishingly, it looks much the same as it did when he saw it. Lake and river, many thousands of miles of shoreline are unbroken by human structures and are horizoned only with the tips of spruce. The lakes are still necklaced with dry-ki, some of it more than a century old. Dry-ki has come to be regarded as charming. It certainly makes good firewood, a smokeless fire.

After forty-odd miles of Penobscot River, we are impatient

for a change. For all its big bends and deadwaters—larger dimensions the farther we go—the river is now hemming us in, and we anticipate Chesuncook Lake, a burst of space. The skyline is opening up some. The lake must be around the next, or the next, bend. Thoreau said that in this same reach of the river he found himself approaching the big lake "with as much expectation as if it had been a university." The river debouches. The lake breaks open. We move out onto it and look to the right down miles of water and far beyond to the high Katahdin massif. Katahdin is a mile high. The lake's elevation is less than a thousand feet. Katahdin stands alone. The vast terrain around it is the next thing to a peneplain. Wherever you paddle through this country, when you move out onto the big lakes you can look to the southeast and see Katahdin.

A steady wind is blowing from the direction of the mountain, and since we are heading north we hold the canoes together and put up an improvised sail. Supported by two paddles as masts, the sail is the largest plastic bag I have ever seen —five by five feet. It is something called a Gaylord liner and comes from the small plastics factory in Greenville, where both Blanchettes work. The canoes move smartly before the wind. Indians used great sheets of bark as sails, and moose hide as well. According to *The Bark Canoes and Skin Boats of North America*, Indians of prehistory "may have set up a leafy bush in the bow of their canoes to act as a sail with favorable winds." At any rate, "the old Nova Scotia expression 'carrying too much bush,' meaning over-canvassing a boat, is thought by some to have originated from an Indian practice observed there by the first settlers." Thoreau sailed using a blanket. Our plastic sail sets Henri Vaillancourt off on a long, surprising tirade against the mills and factories of Greenville, which he says are sweatshops, exploiters of immigrant labor. "I'm glad I don't have to work in one of those places," he says.

The Survival of the Bark Canoe

"Particularly that plastics shop. What a rip-off!" For Mike, the plastics shop is a summer job. He is a student at the University of New Hampshire. His brother, Rick, who is already a college graduate, wants to be a librarian in a New England college. He works full time in the plastics shop and also takes graduate courses in library science at Fitchburg State. Water rushes by and between the canoes. Holding the polyethylene sail, Rick quotes one of his favorite lines from Thoreau, which was occasioned by Thoreau's first night here on Chesuncook. He had moose meat for dinner and afterward went for a walk. "For my dessert," he said, and Rick is now quoting him, "I helped myself to a large slice of the Chesuncook woods, and took a hearty draught of its waters with all my senses."

Vaillancourt sneers. "Some dessert," he says. "Thoreau was a great guy, but a little far-flung there at times. What a crackpot—a real featherbrain, a very impractical person."

Blanchette is annoyed. Vaillancourt is amused. Blanchette says, "Yes? Well, the most influential man of this century will turn out to be Thoreau, who lived in the century before."

"He was extreme," Vaillancourt goes on. "He would not cut down a live tree. You can use nature without destroying it. I have an aunt in Concord. I asked her what people there thought of Thoreau, and she said, 'He was a real bum.'"

"Thoreau actually started a couple of forest fires in his time," Blanchette admits. "One in Concord. The other on Mt. Washington. When the fires went out of control, Thoreau just walked away."

"He said he thought he could make a bark canoe," Vaillancourt adds. "I doubt very much if he could have. That Aitteon, for an Indian, didn't know much, either. Thoreau asked him about the canoe, how the ribs were attached to the gunwales, and he said, 'I don't know. I never noticed.' Aitteon saw a porcupine once and thought it was a bear."

The Gaylord liner is pulling us up the west side of Gero, a big island. Near the island shore, Vaillancourt sees two, three, four tall specimen birches, paper birches—perfection trees. He decides in an instant to camp below them tonight.

It is morning now, after a tormented, insectile night. The mosquitoes were the least of it, the no-see-ums infernal. The wind never stirred enough to take them away. No-see-ums are so small they go right through the screening of the tent. They home on flesh. They cover the hands, the arms, the neck, the face. Like an acid, they eat skin. They are not ubiquitous, but they have been with us now two nights in a row. At 3 A.M., I got up and went out of the tent and down to the shore. I went into the water like a fly-crazed moose. I stayed in the lake in the dark for an hour, as I had in the river the night before, only the nose out—dozing.

"No-see-um" was an Indian word—red skin vulnerable as white. To the early Indian, coming here to make a warm-weather camping trip would have seemed the act of a fool: Thoreau, with his veil, his smoke from rotting logs; we, with our Off and our Cutter. When the tribes lived here—before the logging whites came—they left in the summer. When the blackflies, the mosquitoes, and the no-see-ums hatched, the Indians departed, and they did not come back until the bugs were gone. They went to the coast—to what is now Kenne-

---

bunkport, Northeast Harbor, Fortunes Rocks—and there they steamed clams and lobsters in hot seaweed and ate them the summer long. Between feasts, they dried clams and lobsters to take home for the winter. These were thoughts for the night, underwater.

Henri's beef jerky has begun to turn green. He dips it into peanut butter and eats it for breakfast. The one taste envelops the other.

I make my notes as I watch the bread rise in my reflector oven. The dough began as Bisquick, and it is turning golden brown. Last night we had spice cake; gingerbread the night before. In my own porings through *The Maine Woods*, I have found something that has apparently never arrested Henri Vaillancourt's eye. Thoreau refers a couple of times to a cooking device known as a Yankee-baker. ("A shed-shaped tent will catch and reflect the heat like a Yankee-baker, and you may be drying while you are sleeping.") So Thoreau himself would have recognized my reflector oven—an endorsement that might have been helpful when Vaillancourt was saying "hang it up" but is hardly necessary now. Henri likes the gingerbread, and if his beef jerky gets any greener he plans to use the reflector to reroast it. The baker is a small, collapsible lean-to of shining tin, with a shelf in it for holding a rectangular pan. You fill the pan with dough or batter and set the oven close to the fire. Level it. Watch to see that it is not picking up too much or too little heat. It reflects heat into the pan from the interior—back, sides, top, and bottom. Henri's way of cooking Bisquick is to wrap a gluey mass around a green stick and then jab the stick into the ground near the fire. The Blanchettes tried that, and when the Bisquick began to plop off the stick they removed their dough to the baker.

This is a fine campsite, looking north over the water to the end of Chesuncook, and growing here is everything that goes into a bark canoe: feasible birch, dense stands of tall cedar, hard maple, white pine, white and black spruce. Henri would like to contrive to be put in the Maine woods someday (dropped in, somehow, out of nowhere) without a canoe or a paddle but with some food and gear and just three tools: an axe, an awl, and a crooked knife. He says they are everything he would need in order—three weeks later—to paddle out in a new canoe. This island is the sort of place where he could do it, and that is why he has stopped here, to take a long, wistful look around.

After unloading his canoe last night, he went straight to one of the big birches and took a sample of its bark. He cut it from near the base of the trunk—a piece six inches high and a foot long, the size of a shingle. Along the grain he bent the sample, steadily applying pressure with his fingers as the bark formed the shape of a U. Gradually, he increased the pressure until the bark cracked. It was pretty good bark, he said. It had good relative elasticity. Its layers did not tend to separate. In these respects, as in others, bark will vary a great deal from tree to tree. The eyes—the dotted lines that run in the direction of the grain—were not too close together. The closer the eyes, the weaker the bark. He cut a sample from another tree, with the same results. The third birch he came to was better still—a remarkably straight and columnar tree, with a usable segment of bark that was long enough in itself for a sixteen-foot canoe. Henri said, "There are trees in the White Mountains that put these trees to shame. For Maine, though, these are all right. They're acceptable trees."

He finds his bark, usually, in the White Mountains, and in New Hampshire woods that are north of the White Mountains, and in forests of southwestern Maine. He leaves his car by the side of the road and wanders through the woods—searching, sampling. The trees have to be clean-lined and free of blemishes. The slightest, barely detectable bend in a trunk will cause puckers—welts—in the bark of a finished canoe. He walks on sometimes for many miles, looking not just for good trees but for good big trees. A single tree once gave him two fourteen-foot canoes and most of an eighteen-footer as well. When he finds the sort of quality he is looking for, appreciation registers in his mind and he moves on. These are scouting trips. He will return for the bark when he needs it. He remembers regretfully the best white birch he ever saw. "It was like a palm tree, it was so straight." When he was ready for the bark and went back for it, all he found was a stump. A timber company had taken the tree for spindles and spools. No matter how far off in the woods a tree may be, he does not mark its location on a map or otherwise assist his memory. "When you are in this business, a good birch will make an impression on you," he says. "You remember where it is."

His range has increased, and so has his capacity for guessing where to look. "I've been finding better bark in recent years," he says. "Better bark, that's for damned sure."

I ask him where.

"Near Canada," he says.

"Where near Canada?"

"I don't want to mention too specifically where I get the bark."

"Why not?"

"I just don't care to, that's all."

"Are you worried about the law?"

"The law? Oh, no. Oh hell, no."

"So, what is it that troubles you?"

"I don't want anyone horning in on my birch. If there's one thing I'm possessive about, it's where the good bark is. I wouldn't sell a sheet of good bark for anything—even for a price greater than the price of the canoe I could make from it."

When he goes to take the bark from a tree, he enters the forest with a wooden ladder. He slits the bark vertically and

The Survival of the Bark Canoe

begins to peel it back. If the month is June or early July, the bark will "almost pop off by itself"—will, at any rate, easily come free. Bark taken at this time of the year is called summer bark, and on a canoe it gradually turns a lighter and lighter brown, until it is high buff. Bark that is peeled before the sap flows is called winter bark, and on a canoe it gradually turns a darker and darker brown, until it is a rich cordovan. Canoe coverings usually include several pieces of bark, and they can be attractively quilted with mixtures of the two kinds, as are the hulls of both of our canoes.

"Winter bark is really tight, I'm telling you. You need a special tool, a type of spud, to get it off."

Henri makes the peeling tool from bark itself—stiff bark with a bevelled edge. With much effort, he—in effect—chisels the winter bark off the tree. Winter or summer, when he is done he has something like a long piece of linoleum. He rolls it up the short way, brown side out. Norwegians roof houses with birch bark. Lapps make clothing with it. In Siberia, birch bark has been found—unchanged through all the centuries since it grew—clinging to petrified wood. Henri's long searches are not the result of a modern scarcity of appropriate trees. The search always took time. Indians spent as much as a week roving birch-filled woods looking for a perfect tree. Henri ties the roll of bark with a pine root, or with a length of spruce or cedar bark, or with his belt or a string. He shoulders the ladder and walks out of the woods, leaving behind him a standing but slaughtered tree.

The parts of a bark canoe—in the general order in which they are assembled—are these:

center thwart   ——

quarter thwarts (2)   ——

end thwarts (2)

inwales (2)

wedges
pegs
bark
split roots of black spruce or white pine
outwales (2)
wulegessis (2)
stempieces (2)
pitch
planking
ribs (40 or 50)
headboards (2)
dry cedar shavings or dry moss
gunwale caps (2)
porcupine quills (optional)

Inwales and outwales are collectively called gunwales. The inwale, a strip of cedar running the length of the canoe, is about an inch and a half square in the center and tapers toward the ends. The outwale is a thinner strip and also runs the length of the canoe. The edge of the bark and the tips of the ribs are pinched between the inwale and the outwale.

The *wulegessis* is a flap of bark that forms a deck over the bow (or the stern) and extends a short way down the sides of the canoe.

The headboards are ovate slabs of cedar that are wedged vertically into the bow and the stern to contribute both support and form.

If Henri were to build a canoe here on Gero Island, he would start by felling cedar, splitting it out, and whittling and forming various parts. He would cut young birch or maple for thwarts. Always, he prepares the wooden pieces first. Ribs, planking, stempieces, gunwales, and headboards are made from cedar. After carving rib boards in varying lengths, he dips them in boiling water and then bends them around his knee to an appropriate shape, which, for the center of the canoe, is much like the letter C lying on its back. To hold the tension and the shape, he ties a strip of cedar bark from tip to tip, and a rib is made. As the ribs progress from the center of the canoe toward the ends, they must become not only shorter but also more sharply bent. Some are actually cracked a bit to approach the shape of a V. He racks up several dozen subtly graduated ribs, like auto parts awaiting delivery to an assembly line.

That is the building bed—a section of ground about twenty feet long, free of rocks and roots. The soil has to be firm enough to hold driven stakes. If the bed is level, the canoe will come off it with a slight rocker in the profile of the bottom. Henri likes it that way, and here on the island he would clear a level bed.

No one knows how the canoe's design began, centuries ago. I venture to guess that the structure of the hull was modelled on the thoracic structure of vertebrates—of men and animals, reptiles and birds. The skin is bark. The flesh is planking. A cage of bent-cedar ribs gives the craft its skeletal form. Between a wood-and-canvas canoe and a bark canoe there is an elemental difference in the order in which the hull is assembled. In the more modern canoe, the canvas comes last. It is stretched across an essentially completed and rigid frame. The Indian, on the other hand, began the assembly with bark. He rolled it right out on the building bed, white side up, and built the canoe from there. Lashing the bark to the gunwale frame, he made—in effect—an elongated birch-bark bag. Then he lined the bag with planking. Then—one by one—he forced in the ribs. The resulting canoe was lithe, supple, resilient, strong. And if something cracked, it could easily be replaced.

When, at the outset, the bark was folded upward from the building bed, a template was needed to guide the bark toward the shape of a canoe. The Indians used two kinds of template. The one gave the canoe bulging tumblehome sides. The other made the sides flare. Henri Vaillancourt uses both kinds. The template that will lead to pronounced tumblehome is actually the completed gunwale frame of the canoe itself— all thwarts in place, mortised into the inwales, which are lashed together at the ends. The gunwale frame (looked at from above) is the outline of the intended canoe. The other kind of template, which does not end up as part of the canoe, is called a building frame and is simply a smaller (shorter and narrower) version of the gunwale frame.

Henri places on the building bed whatever frame he is using and drives stakes into the ground in outline around it. He removes the stakes. He rolls out the bark, white side up. He sets the frame on top of the bark. He centers it—bark protruding on all sides—and he tries as best he can to line up the frame with the stake holes below, which are now hidden by the bark. Satisfied, he weights down the frame with rocks.

The bark that protrudes outside the frame is to be bent upward, but it cannot be bent without forming pronounced wrinkles. So, from the edges, wedge-shaped indentations—gores —are cut into it in a number of places to within an inch of the frame. Then the bark is folded upward all around the frame. As the builder works along, he puts the stakes back into their holes, and when all stakes are in place they form a confining palisade around the upturned bark, which has now begun to assume the appearance of a canoe—ragged, lumpy, flat-bottomed, but still a canoe. A much greater breadth of bark is required in the middle, of course, than at the ends, so, unless the bark came from a tree of extraordinary girth, the sides of the canoe for several feet amidships have to be "pieced out" with additional bark, which Henri now sews on with split roots.

It is better that all this happen in good shade, which is deep and abundant here on Gero Island, because in direct sunlight the bark becomes less flexible, and it needs all the elasticity it can retain during the building process. Indians would choose a site like this—with its available water, shade, and materials— and build canoe after canoe in the one place for many generations.

As Henri works, he is not worried about an irretrievable error. Nothing can go so disastrously wrong that he has no alternative but to junk the whole thing and begin again. "Nothing about it is, you know, that dramatic," he says. The Indian methodology was in no sense haphazard, and a canoe will result every time if the method has been understood and mastered. Within tolerable margins, the results do vary, however, and no two canoes are alike. Some, in the end, please him more than others. "They don't always come out exactly the way you want them to."

The bark is clamped to the surrounding palisade of stakes by short half-rounds of wood tied to the stakes with strips peeled from basswood. Pinched between stake and half-round, the birch bark will stay put while the gunwale frame is lashed in its proper place. The gunwale frame, now lifted a foot or so off the ground in the center, and more at the ends, is temporarily supported by wooden posts that have been cut to varying lengths so they will establish the profile curve of the gunwales—the upsweep toward the ends, the sheer of the canoe. When the sheer is just right, the deck flaps—*wulegessis*—are placed on the ends, the outwales are added (secured by pegs that go through the bark and into the inwales), and lashing of the gunwales begins. The split roots go around the gunwales and through awl holes in the bark, around, around, around again, each pass snug beside another. It is necessary, however, to do this in groups—to stop the lashing, leave a space, and start again, for the space eventually accommodates the tip of a rib, poking up between inwale and outwale. The grouped lashings, handsome to look at, are evenly spaced along both gunwales. The decorative dividend is high. The gunwale lashings contribute considerably to the beauty of the canoe. Yet they are vital and, in pattern, completely functional.

The canoe is about ready to come off the building bed. Stakes have been removed while the lashing progressed. The edges of the gores are sewn together, making neat seams. The thwarts, which are mortised into the gunwales, are further secured by lashings that run through awl holes near their ends. The canoe is lifted, turned upside down, and placed on wooden horses. Lumpish and battered-looking, it appears to be covered not so much with smooth birch bark as with parts of a used tin roof. The canoe is so crooked that it is difficult even to guess where the centerline might be. The stempieces are now tied in, and they at least suggest the profiles of the ends. Wherever sewing remains undone, it is completed. The canoe is then set on the ground again, upright—ready to be gummed, planked, and ribbed.

Inside the hull, all seams are "payed with gum." Indian gum was mainly the pitch of white or black spruce. Indians tapped trees in a way analogous to the collection of maple sap; they boiled the pitch and strained it, and at tribal campgrounds they had communal pitch pots where anyone could go for sealant to touch up a canoe. Henri Vaillancourt has used spruce gum on a number of his canoes, but his preference of late has been to use mineral pitch—plain asphalt roofing cement. Asphalt and dark spruce pitch are almost identical to the eye and the touch, but there is an incongruity here that I cannot to my own satisfaction resolve. Why would someone who had used spruce gum with the same good results the Indians got, someone who would drive hundreds of miles and then walk tens of miles to select a single tree, someone who would disdain power tools and elect to work twelve hours a day with an axe and a crooked knife, someone who would put no metal in a canoe whatsoever (not so much as a carpet tack), although Indians used nails in their canoes even before 1850, someone who would travel to outposts of Ontario just in the hope of learning a detail or two from an Indian, someone to whom authenticity was an otherwise primal value—an artist, for that by style and temperament is what he is—seal his canoes with mineral pitch? His own (quick) answer is that he would unhesitatingly use anything—nails, wire, buzz saws, vinyl tile—that might be an improvement on Indian materials or technology, but for canoe-making nothing modern *is* an improvement, except, in a small way, asphalt, because to collect and boil spruce pitch involves unnecessary tedium. Whether the pitch is vegetable or mineral, the seams of bark canoes have to be touched up with some frequency. The Indians mixed animal fat into the spruce gum to keep it from cracking in cold weather, and they had to be careful to repitch their canoes in warm weather so the pitch would not weep. With all this, Henri won't be bothered. So he carries in his pack a small pan that contains a cupful of hard asphalt.

As planking and ribs are installed, a bark canoe takes its

final form. The planking—also called sheathing—lines the bark: fifteen (or so) random-width cedar boards running from each end to the middle, and overlapping there by about six inches. Pressure from the ribs is all that holds the planking in place. Temporary ribs—bent saplings, or ribs rejected in the making of other canoes—are used to hold the planking before the permanent ribs are installed. Nearly three weeks have by now gone into the assembly of the canoe, and the time of completion has come, as fifty ribs, give or take a few, are pounded into position with a mallet. "I've heard one or two people call them 'floating ribs,'" Henri says. "They're not anchored. They can move a little. You work from the ends toward the middle, putting the ribs in. You pour very hot water on the bark to keep it flexible at this stage." To install a rib, it is necessary to tilt it a bit and put its tips in place in the gunwales. Then the rib is firmly tapped with the mallet, and as it moves toward the vertical it presses ever more tightly against the planking and the bark. If the rib is too large, it will split the bark. If it is too small, it will not offer the pressure needed to create and maintain the hull form. Where a rib is not quite right, Henri tries another. When he taps the last one in, it is below the center thwart.

He trims the bark at the ends and sews roots around the stempieces. He fills out the bow and stern by stuffing them with shavings or moss, kept in place by the headboards, which are installed next. He pegs on the gunwale caps—long, narrow strips of cedar that cover the top of the gunwales and protect the grouped lashings from wear. He turns the canoe over again and pitches the seams on the outside. The canoe is done now—ready to take its maker home from an island in Maine, or the reverse, whichever the case may be. All that is left is to find a porcupine. Take some quills. Commence the decorations.

When white explorers first came to northeastern North America, they looked in wonder at such canoes—as well they might, for nothing like them existed in Europe. There was eloquence in the evidence they gave of the genius of human-kind. The materials were simple, but the structure was not. An adroit technology had come down with the tribes from im-memorial time, and now—in the sixteenth, the seventeenth century—here were bark canoes on big rivers and ocean bays curiously circling ships from another world. Longboats were lowered, to be rowed by crews of four and upward. The sailors hauled at their oars. The Indians, two to a canoe, indolently whisked their narrow paddles and easily drew away. In their wake they left a stunning impression. Not only were they faster. They could see where they were going.

White explorers got out of their ships and went thousands of miles in bark canoes. They travelled in them until the twen-tieth century, for bark canoes were the craft of the north con-tinent. Nothing else, indigenous or imported, could do what they could do. The explorers in the main were not seeking the advancement of geophysical knowledge, chimeric routes to the Orient. They were looking for fur. Fur sources around the Baltic Sea were diminishing, and prices there had risen to prohibitive levels, so the attention of Western Europe had turned to the American woods. The demand for fur was intense, because it was used not only in pelt form but also, and to a much greater extent, in the making of felt and other materials. Most wanted of all was the fur of the beaver. The underhair, or "beaver wool," had minute barbs, and when the hair was compressed the barbs would hold fabric together.

The fur trade began in the estuaries of rivers. White traders soon followed the Indians upstream to complete their transactions nearer the sources of the fur. What the whites brought to offer were not merely clothes, blankets, beads, and copper kettles but also steel traps, spears, knives, and guns, with which the Indians could vastly increase the collection of fur. Red and white hands were clasped in enterprise. Some Canadians savor the thought that while Americans to the south—intoxicated with their "Manifest Destiny"—were killing Indians and stealing their land, Canadians red and white were developing warm interracial relationships bonded by a business that was conducted to the advantage of all. All but the beaver. Where Indian families might once have taken just a few pelts for their own use, whole lodges were destroyed. Beaver populations declined toward zero with proximity to the outlets of commerce. Thus the Ojibway, the Cree, the Algonquin—Canadian tribes across the woods—were in on the beginnings of the end of their own environment. They were willing partners, profiteers. Down the river they sold the beaver, the mink, the marten, the lynx, the otter. They sold the hides of deer, moose, caribou. They even sold the skin of the wild goose. They sold anything with hair, almost anything that moved—and to keep the whole bonanza going they sold their birch canoes.

The fur trade, as it lengthened, manifested its own destiny

and Canada's, too. The fur trade established canoe routes to the far northwest, and conjoined the segments of a continental wilderness. It is possible to cross Canada by canoe, to crisscross Canada, to go almost anywhere. Canada is twenty-five per cent water. The quantity of it outreaches belief. A sixth of all the fresh water that exists on earth is in Canadian lakes, Canadian ponds, Canadian streams, Canadian rivers. A friend of mine who grew up in Timmins, a remote community in Ontario, once told me about an Indian friend of his in boyhood who developed an irresistible urge to see New York City. He put his canoe in the water and started out. From stream to lake to pond to portage, he made his way a hundred miles to Lake Timiskaming, and its outlet, the Ottawa River. He went down the Ottawa to the St. Lawrence, down the St. Lawrence to the Richelieu, up the Richelieu to Lake Champlain, and from Lake Champlain to the Hudson. At the Seventy-ninth Street Boat Basin, he left the canoe in the custody of attendants and walked on into town. Reversing that trip, and then some, one could go by canoe from Seventy-ninth Street to Alaska, and down the Yukon to the Bering Sea. By the Rat-Porcupine route (up the Rat, down the Porcupine), the length of the portage over the Rocky Mountains is half a mile. Between the Atlantic and the Pacific, anywhere on the routes that were used by the fur trade, the longest portage is thirteen miles (and even that is an exaggeration, because the trail is interrupted by a mile-long lake). In 1778, a white trader for the first time crossed that portage. It is Methye Portage, in what is now northern Saskatchewan. His name was Peter Pond. Beyond the portage, in the region of Lake Athabasca, he encountered a crowded population of beaver whose fur (as a result of the mean temperature there) was as long and rich as any yet found in North America. The discovery extended to its practical limit the distance that fur could travel in the unfrozen season by canoe from the source to Montreal. Transatlantic ships could navigate the St. Lawrence to the Lachine Rapids, near Montreal. At the head of the rapids, the fur-trade canoe routes began. The distance from Lachine to Lake Athabasca was three thousand miles. Unsurprisingly, the men who did the paddling were known as the *voyageurs*.

Some stayed in the far-northern outposts for the winter, others in Montreal. With the spring breakup, they started from both ends, and by midsummer had met in the middle. They exchanged cargoes. These were some of the things in the packs bound west and north: false hair, garters, tomahawks, rolls of bark from the birches of the East. The *voyageurs* returned—the survivors returned—whence they had come. Crosses marked their routes, sometimes many crosses in a single place. Packs weighed ninety pounds, and a *voyageur* on a portage was responsible for six. Generally, two packs were portaged at a time, and sometimes three. The largest recorded burden carried by one man in one trip across a portage was six hundred and thirty pounds. It has been reported that the *voyageurs* liked to show off. They were, on the whole, small men; large ones were not worth their extra weight in fur. Even under the hundred-and-eighty-pound weight of a standard two-pack load, they were more or less forced to run if they wanted to move at all, so they took off at a trot at the start of a portage—uphill, downhill, over rough or boggy terrain. They died of strangulated hernias, and of heart attacks, sometimes. Five hundred mink skins would fit in one pack. *Voyageurs* also drowned in rapids.

When they started out in the spring from Montreal, they were blessed by a priest, and each canoe was given a summer-ration eight-gallon keg of brandy. The *voyageurs* drank most of it the first night out. They went virtually nowhere the next day. Sober again, they sang their way to Lake Superior. All day, they sang *chansons* of the Loire Valley, which gave them their rhythm and their distraction. They went up the Ottawa and up the Mattawa and across the Height of Land. They went down the French River from Lake Nipissing to Georgian Bay. They circled the north rim of Lake Superior. They averaged fifty miles a day. When rivers became too shallow for paddling, they shoved upcurrent with poles. When they could not pole, they got out and lined—hauled the canoes, bargelike, from the shore with ropes. When they could not line, they dragged. They would do anything to avoid a portage or reduce its length. There were more than a hundred portages between Lake Athabasca and Montreal.

They wore plumed hats, billowing shirts, bright-colored sashes. Their paddle blades were brilliant red, green, blue. They stopped once an hour for a churchwarden smoke, and they measured big lakes not in miles but in pipes. They got up in the morning at two or three. Hours of paddling preceded breakfast. They made their camp at nine, even ten, at night. In the north, they ate pemmican—pounded buffalo or caribou meat, sometimes with berries in it, dried in the sun. In the Middle West, they ate wild rice and maize. Toward the East, they ate pork and hardtack, peas and beans.

They came in large numbers from the Quebecois farm country east of Montreal, like the forebears of Henri Vaillancourt. From the fur trade the *voyageurs* got almost nothing but a change of scene, in a business that for its owners was unimaginably profitable. An investment of, say, eight hundred pounds could bring back sixteen thousand. The *voyageurs* worked for the North West Company and, ultimately, for the Hudson's Bay Company, which merged the North West Company out of existence in 1821.

Bark canoes the Indians made for themselves seldom exceeded twenty feet, and were generally shorter than that, on down to nine-foot and ten-foot hunter canoes. Canoes they built on order for the fur trade were thirty-six feet long and could carry four tons. It took four men to portage them. Wet, they weighed six hundred pounds. They were known as *canots de maître*. They travelled in brigades—usually four, but sometimes as many as ten, in a line. The bowman, the *avant*, had the captain role. In white water, the sternman, the *gouvernail*, was too far back to see what the *voyageurs* called the *fil d'eau* —the place to shoot the rapid. Paddlers in the middle worked two abreast. Personnel shifts (advancement, transfer, death) caused a crew to vary considerably, and as many as fifteen men sometimes paddled a *canot de maître*. Eight or ten was the usual number. The crew slept under the overturned canoe and an attached tarpaulin, and to make this arrangement as spacious as possible the canoes were designed with high, curling ends. For the more northerly runs through what is now Manitoba and Saskatchewan, the trade developed the *canot du nord*, which was narrower and shorter—twenty-five feet. Some of the streams of the northern route were too small for the *canot de maître*. The companies appropriated the art from the Indians, set up their own factories, and made bark canoes. On spruce-plank building beds with permanent stake holes, the plant at Trois-Rivières, Quebec, could produce in a year twenty *canots de maître*. Certain white names ultimately acquired celebrity in the field, notably L. A. Christopherson, who for almost forty years built, and in part designed, Hudson's Bay Company fur-trade canoes. High on their curling sterns were the letters "HBC." This, in company argot, meant "Here Before Christ."

Inevitably, after working for some years in the sixteen-foot range, Henri Vaillancourt developed an ambition to build a fur-trade canoe. He needed an order, though. It was not the sort of thing he could just stop and do, since he was laden with commitments and was taking orders a year and more ahead. Meanwhile, on a reconnaissance trip in northern New Hampshire he had found one of the largest birches he had ever seen. It had suitable, elastic bark. He decided not to use the bark for sixteen-foot canoes. It would stay there on the living tree until he got an order for a *canot du nord,* or even a *canot de maître.*

All through his building history, Vaillancourt has experimented with aspects of the craft, going through phases that have been less pragmatic than artistic in their shifts and choices. Some of his early canoes were very sharp-ended. "I had a thing for sharp ends," he explains. "The sharp-ended ones were fast canoes. They looked good." They were narrow in the bow and stern to the point of seeming hollow-cheeked. It was difficult to turn them. They could not be called responsive. They cut a fine, deep line into the water, and straight ahead was the direction in which they wanted to go. Compared with an apple-cheeked Grumman canoe, Henri's canoes still look like cutlery, but of late the ends have markedly amplified. Why? "I like it that way. I think it looks good." The criterion is always the same: "It looks good." His canoes were once narrower in beam as well. They have always been shallow —rarely deeper than a foot. He has generally preferred straight profiles at the ends. "But sometimes I'll give it some heel toward the bottom, or undercut it a little bit. It depends on your mood when you build it." He used to overlap his planking, like clapboard, in the Abnaki manner. Then, some years ago, in his travels he saw a Malecite canoe with edge-to-edge planking. "It was so neat-looking. So sophisticated. I just had to do it. It's much harder to do." With the edge-to-edge planking, he began making wider and thicker ribs. They look good against the planking.

The largest canoe dealer in the East uses a Vaillancourt canoe as a conversation piece in a showroom full of Old Towns. A woman named Jean Newton, who lives in a shed in the Palouse mountains of Idaho, has a Vaillancourt tumble-home canoe that was made from a single piece of bark. She saw Henri's name in *The Last Whole Earth Catalog,* to which he once wrote a letter promoting trade. Her canoe hangs from the shed rafters, on cinches. The canoe Henri is using on this trip was ordered by Idaho State University for a course on Indian canoeing and for the making of an educational film. John Farrell, of Warren, New Jersey, discovered Henri in the "Small Business & Crafts" section of *Yankee* magazine and ordered a fourteen-foot Vaillancourt canoe, which he uses for fishing and duck hunting on the upper Passaic River. Warren Soderberg, who owns a hardware store in Dresser, Wisconsin, bought an eighteen-foot Vaillancourt canoe so that, among other things, he could make fifteen-day canoe trips in Ontario during moose season in the fall. "I'd like to shoot a moose out of my birch-bark canoe with a bow and arrow," he said. "Why? Just to say that I've done it." Henri made a nine-foot hunter canoe for a woman in New Jersey who wanted one that small so she could lift it herself. It weighs twenty pounds.

Then, finally, an order came for a fur-trade canoe. The customer's name was Kent Reeves. He lived in Shokan, New York, and he was a professor of environmental education whose classroom was a forest (called the Ashokan Field Campus). It belonged to a subdivision of the State University. Reeves had conceived, and was in the process of organizing, a graduate course that would be one long field trip on the route of the *voyageurs*, mainly west of Superior. It would be called Frontier Life on the Voyageurs' Trail—six credits toward a master's degree. Beyond Reeves' considerable library on the fur-trade era, what the course needed most was a *canot du nord*. Reeves had sought out the names of people who could make one. He had visited them and had examined their work. He had arrived at an opinion of Henri that exactly coincided with Henri's opinion of himself: Henri was, by a considerable margin, the best. The two main considerations that brought Reeves to this conclusion were, in his words, "quality and authenticity." Henri wanted three thousand dollars. Reeves flinched, but he produced the money. The students who signed up for the course made their own paddles, sawing them out of basswood and finishing them with drawknives. They sewed their own billowy shirts and wove bright-colored sashes. They made *voyageur* hats, and they made moccasins with moose skin from the HBC. Meanwhile, Henri made the *canot du nord*. The bark was all it had appeared to be when it stood in the forest, and the canoe was representative of the best work he could do. He was still tapping in ribs as the course was about to begin, and the day he finished the canoe someone sent by Reeves arrived to take it away. Henri could not stand to see it go, and he was in an ugly mood for the rest of the summer. Finished in the morning, gone in the afternoon—never again would he let that happen, he decided. He was never going to be deadlined by a day, or even a month —the year alone was enough of a promise. He wanted his canoes around for a while when they were done. Wistfully, he wondered if the North Canoe would ever come back to Greenville for a touchup in "the yard." Meanwhile, in the Quetico-Superior, it went up the Pigeon River on the route of the *voyageurs*. It was poled upstream and lined up rapids. It was a dry, sound, stable canoe—beautiful in sheer, smoothly seamed, with high, Christopherson ends. The graduate students sprayed themselves with Off and carried freeze-dried food, but they also learned and sang Loire Valley songs, ate some pork and dried peas, and drank from eight-gallon kegs of brandy. The course, moving northward, was a total success. It established itself in the curriculum. It left nothing in its wake but a lonely master of arts.

Henri Vaillancourt once had a dead bear in his room at college. This emerges as we move north on the northernmost arm of Chesuncook Lake. Between the canoes, idle conversation is for us what the *chansons* were for the *voyageurs*. Up at six, we have been on the water since seven-forty-five. The wind has not yet come up for the day. The canoes tend to separate. One or the other moves wide or falls behind. The gap extends until it reaches a kind of psychological apogee, at which moment binding forces begin to apply, and the two canoes—alone on hundreds of acres of water—draw slowly together until they all but touch.

Rick Blanchette says to Henri, when the gap is narrow, "So. How are you?"

"Fine. How are you? Still working down at the plastics shop?"

"Yes. Still building canoes?"

"Yes."

"How are the wife and kids?" Henri has no wife and kids.

"Fine. How are *your* wife and kids?"

Rick has none, either, but this ritual occurs at least twice a day.

I have told them they sound like Kordofan Arabs, who say to one another:

"God bless you."

"How is your health?"

"Thanks be to God, well."

"God bless you."

"How are your camels?"

"Thanks be to God, well. How are your camels?"

"Thanks be to God, well. How are your cattle?"

"Thanks be to God, well." And so on through any living thing in sight or mind.

And now Henri says to Rick, "How are your camels?"

And Rick says, "Thanks be to God, well. How are your cattle?"

And—to put a stop to it—I say, "God bless you. How is your dead bear?"

Henri explains that it was a cub and did not take up much space in the room.

"A *cub!*" Warren Elmer says, and his paddle stops.

"Someone had shot it, and my roommate got it from a butcher. I wanted to have the skin."

"I'd like to have the skin of the person who shot it," Warren says, and with his paddle rips a hole in the lake.

"If someone shot it, you know, someone might as well make use of it," Henri says, with a dismissive shrug. The gap begins to widen again. He takes the lead. He likes to be in the lead. He crosses our bow—so close that we have to stop to let him pass.

There has been an inordinate amount of talk this morning about Mud Pond Carry, which is only a mile or so ahead of us, and which comes back into the conversation now as we make the first portage of the trip—although "portage" is hardly the word for it. A scant fifty feet separates Chesuncook Lake from Umbazooksus Stream, across the low remains of an earth-fill logging dam. The topographic map indicates that Mud Pond Carry, two miles long, is a straight walk with a gentle rise of seventy feet followed by a gentle drop of sixty. There is tension, though, in Henri's voice when he talks about it, and in Rick's as well—a lot of verbal flexing and dancing around, with tremors at the mention of the name. I don't understand why. Perhaps it is because Thoreau got lost there—wandered right off into the woods, and was found, by his guide, many miles away.

We move on up Umbazooksus Stream, which is almost a deadwater—a current so light it can scarcely bend grass. We have come into a quiet, somewhat eerie chamber in the woods. Inaccurately, it puts forth a sense of lurking harm, and someone mentions *Deliverance*. We have all read the book or seen the movie—about four men on a canoe trip, one of whom is sexually abused at gunpoint by a stubbly-bearded mountain man—and among us *Deliverance* has become a sort of standing joke, like the plastics shop and the camels. *Deliverance* may have been set at the far end of the Appalachian chain, but its thought-wave effects seem to have reached to wherever canoes may float, and in one way or another we have all been warned not to go on canoe trips. Were we crazy? Did we realize what could *happen* out there? Had we seen *Deliverance?*

James Dickey, author of the novel and of the script of the film, lives on an artificial lake in Columbia, South Carolina. He teaches creative writing at the university there. He owns an aluminum canoe, and, by the report of colleagues, has logged in it journeys of impressively short distance. Students gather around him, and he says, "We need white water!," and they address the canoe to the shore of the flat brown lake. Dickey goes into the house and comes back with a half-gallon bottle of bourbon, glasses, and ice. He goes in again, and comes out with his bow and arrow, his Martin guitar, and more duffel and cargo, until the canoe, loaded and launched, is low in the freeboard with students, writer, and gear. The canoe goes over the water. Then the water goes over the canoe. The canoe rolls, spills everyone. The guitar floats away. Dickey struggles to his feet. The lake comes up to his knees.

Such germinal scenes, transmuted in the treasuries of the author's imagination, have led to the impression that this mildest, gentlest, safest of outdoor activities—pursued for generations by summering teachers and Explorer Scouts—is a fearshot thing to do. We decide that Umbazooksus Stream is James Dickey country, and around the next bend we will encounter the Umbazooksus Stationary Rapist, who, truth be told, is flown in each day from Boston. With thumbless hands, he strums a banjo while he waits.

From time to time, we encounter on the rivers and lakes other people in canoes. Warren and I, on a long walk in the woods one day in the hope of seeing wildlife, see instead two travelling canoemen in yellow slickers drinking canned beer by their beached canoe. As we emerge from the woods and walk toward them, incredible fear comes into their eyes. We are hairy—I with a stubble, Warren with a Visigoth's beard. We have no apparent canoe. We look "native" enough to rape a stone. One of the men has cherubic cheeks and fair hair and a fat tummy and small eyes, and he seems to be aware of his unfortunate resemblance to the victim in *Deliverance*. The closer we move, the beadier the eyes become. The beer can is up like plasma. We are now on top of these men, and there is nothing warm in their regard, which seems to say, "One more step and we'll scream."

"Hello," Warren says.

"Hi," I insert.

Warren speaks to them of routes and the weather. It is at once apparent that he has been miscast. His voice is all wrong to bear freight of danger, ignoble tones of any kind. The beer descends. The eyes de-bead. The scene uncreates itself.

Facts fulfill fiction sometimes, though. The river in the South that is most often identified as *Deliverance* country has attracted many hundreds of people who might otherwise have never in their lives stepped into a canoe. With some apparent sense of secondhand macho and shared novelistic experience, they have set out in canoes on the river; and, like boys from Hotchkiss and Groton being gored in the streets of Pamplona, a few of them have been killed—the ultimate adventure—but not by the gun of a strange aggressor. They have been killed by fast-moving water, with which their experience was limited to having seen it on film.

Dickey is not responsible, of course. He did not create foolhardiness. All he created was an imaginative book full of wildly impossible canoeing scenes—canoes diving at steep angles down breathtaking cataracts, and shooting like javelins through white torrents among blockading monoliths—and a film that was faithful to the book. A canoe trip is a society so small and isolated that its frictions—and everything else about it—can magnify to stunning size. When trouble comes on a canoe trip, it comes from the inside, from fast-growing hatreds among the friends who started. Perhaps Dickey delivered less than he might have when he brought trouble in from the outside.

Henri says that his reaction to *Deliverance*, while seeing the movie, was that he couldn't care less who was doing what to whom but he was shocked and alarmed by what was happening to the canoes.

Dingbat Prouty, a hundred years ago, was a logger who worked in this region of the woods, and one noted day he nearly drowned in a multiple tragedy in fast water, at a pitch on the Penobscot that took the lives of three of his companions. Prouty, swimming to safety, pulled himself up on a huge log that was floating in an eddy, and there he searched his soaked clothing, found his pipe and some tobacco that was dry, and had himself a quiet, contemplative smoke while the corpses went on downriver. "Ain't he a James Dickey bird!" said another logger, who watched him sitting there. The year was 1870. "Now, ain't he a James Dickey bird!" The expression was used to describe any person whose words or actions were filled with striking incongruities; and here, north of the Moosehead, it was universally understood.

We take a clearer look at the stream. If ever there was moose country, it is Umbazooksus Stream—with its broad meanders through fields of sedge, its occasional dead standing trees. The stream is quiet and protected, surrounded by forest. We decide that we are going to see a moose here. We will stop paddling, stop talking, and stay until a moose shows up or the stream freezes. We settle down to wait. Stillness envelops us. It is the stillness of a moose intending to appear.

Thoreau was here on the twenty-seventh of July. Polis, his guide, told him that "Umbazooksus" meant "Much Meadow River." Thoreau described it in his journal as "a very meadowy stream, and deadwater. . . . The space between the woods, chiefly bare meadow . . . is a rare place for moose." He described the sedges, the wool grass, the abundant colonies of common blue flag. The year was 1857, and nothing has discernibly changed since then. "It was unusual for the woods to be so distant from the shore," he continued. "There was quite an echo from them, but when I was shouting in order to awake it, the Indian reminded me that I should scare the moose, which he was looking out for, and which we all wanted to see. The word for echo was Pockadunkquaywayle."

It is, of course, possible that a long brown snout will appear, a rack of antlers—unfortunately, a buck. We have seen no deer, but there are enough around—five per square mile of the

Maine forest. Deer are so suburban, however, that for me they would frankly disturb the atmosphere of this remote northern stream. Deer intensely suggest New Jersey. One of the densest concentrations of wild deer in the United States—fifty per square mile—inhabits the part of New Jersey that, as it happens, I inhabit, too. Deer like people. They like to be near people, and New Jersey has more people per acre than any other state. People move out of the city to a New Jersey town and turn rhapsodic at the sight of deer. They write letters, songs, poems implying that they now live on the edge of wilderness. ("There were *deer* outside the window this morning.") Thoreau mentions a "deer that went a-shopping" in the streets of Bangor, explaining that deer "are more common about the settlements." Deer use the sidewalks in the heart of Princeton. A year or so ago, I saw a buck with a big eight-point rocking-chair rack looking magnificent as he stood between two tractor-trailers in the Frito-Lay parking lot in New Brunswick, New Jersey. When the buckshot season comes, New Jersey's deer know it, and at the sound of the first blast they get up on people's porches or stand around on lawns, waiting it out. The season lasts a week, in December. If the deer are patient, they die of old age. Meanwhile, they love apples. They like alfalfa, soybeans, clover, and lettuce. They like much of the truck in the gardens of man. In long files, they move through woodlots from orchards to gardens to the edges of fields. When the squirrels stop playing on the ground and run up into the trees, the herd is coming, travelling into the wind. A doe appears. Another. Another. Sometimes twenty go by, and then there is a skip in time. Now the main buck, the king of the herd, steps out of the woods. Hunters—watching from cover or from tree stands—will choose a buck in summer and take movies of him through the fall, waiting for December. Deer particularly gravitate to semi-rural research centers, of which there are many around Princeton, spaced like moons through the wooded countryside. The hunters know the size and special characteristics of each herd: the Squibb herd, the Dow Jones herd, the Western Electric herd, the Mobil Oil herd. The Institute for Advanced Study has extensive wood-lots, and the smartest deer on earth are in the Institute herd.

If a deer would degrade this place slightly, a moose, on the other hand, would stir the morning. Our patience endures, though, no more than an hour. Like Thoreau before us, we fail to see a moose on Much Meadow River. Above us, a loon flies, laughing. We move on up the stream to its source—Umbazooksus Lake. A strong north wind has come up, and we have to fight it across the lake to the beginning of the carry.

Henri is edgy before the start. With considerable meticulousness, he slowly ties his tumpline to the center thwart and adjusts his carry board, which is tied to the thwart with a rawhide thong. The tump will fit across his forehead and pick up some of the canoe's weight. The carry board, a flat piece of cedar, a modified shingle, will place weight on the back of his head and the middle of his shoulders. Thoreau described such a carry board in *The Maine Woods*, and Henri has made this one from Thoreau's description. I ask him if the carry board generally helps a lot, and he says he will soon find out.

"You've always done without one?"

"I've never made a portage before."

With the exception of the fifty-foot carry we made into Umbazooksus Stream, he says, this is the first portage of his life.

In astonishment, I ask him, then, how many canoe trips he has made, and he says four—all short ones, and all without portages. I remember the little thirteen-foot canoe he was determined to bring on this trip, and I now understand why. He is well prepared, though, with his tump and carry board, and with two paddles tied to the thwarts so the flat of the blades will rest on his shoulders. He flips the canoe and holds it by the gunwales above him, the bow tip resting on the ground. He lowers the canoe into place on his shoulders. The bow swings upward to a point of balance. He adjusts the tump on his forehead. The over-all rig rides lightly. He starts off fast, almost at a trot, and disappears up the trail. His manual is in his head. "The Indian started off first with the canoe and was soon out of sight, going much faster than an ordinary walk," wrote Thoreau in his journal, describing the start of this portage.

Mud Pond Carry is the way of traffic north, and has been, apparently, since a time soon after the invention of the canoe. So many feet have scuffed across these two miles that the trail is a worn trench, lying well below the surrounding terrain, just as roads in Somerset, many centuries old, run in deep grooves between the fields around them. It is impossible to imagine how Thoreau could have got lost here, how he got out of the long ditch and wandered away, for in his time it was already deep. He called it "a loosely paved gutter" and a "very wet and rocky path through the universal dense evergreen forest . . . where we went leaping from rock to rock and from side to side, in the vain attempt to keep out of the water and mud." If Mud Pond Carry were more ample, we could paddle across it in the canoes, for it is a trail full of water. From one end to the other, bullfrogs live in the portage.

Rick, lighter than Henri and with the heavier canoe, has no tumpline or carry board, and the paddles, almost from the start, cut into his shoulders. With a pack basket and other gear, I walk in front of him and test the footing, so he can avoid following where I sink in deep. The water in the portage is not just standing there in pools. It actually runs—a man-made (foot-made) stream. As we cover the first mile, the current is coming toward us. I keep calling back to Rick, telling him when to step up on "the bank," because the mud is too deep, and when to step back into the trail, because the canoe would otherwise strike the encroaching trees. Now and again, the strain of the canoe's bulk and the knee-wrenching slipperiness underfoot cause him to stop and rest, but he declines all offers of assistance. It is clearly quite important to him that he carry the canoe to the far end by himself. It is his first portage, too.

In the second mile, we notice that the current in the carry is now moving away from us. We have crossed the height of land. The water that ran toward us was on its way to the Penobscot River and Penobscot Bay. The water now running away from us is by nature Allagash flow, headed north to Canada, to go down the St. John to the Bay of Fundy. For some sixty years after Yorktown, Great Britain was under the impression that this height of land was the boundary between the United States and Canada—a viewpoint that contained within it an excuse for war, but the king of Holland was called upon as mediator and the opportunity passed. The king saw the Mud Pond Carry only on a map, and Thoreau thought this a pity, because "the king of Holland would have been in his element" here.

At the Mud Pond end of the carry, Henri combs and recombs his hair. He shows no inclination to go back and get his packs. By conventional procedure, the person not carrying the canoe takes some of the duffel halfway and then goes back for the rest; meanwhile, the canoe carrier goes to the far end, then returns for the gear that has been left at the halfway point. Henri, who has worked out so many of his skills empirically, obviously means to do the same with portaging, and the precedent he sets now is that carrying the canoe is all he will do. Someone else will have to go back for his packs. Warren does so, with a cheerful shrug.

For thirty miles up the Allagash lakes—Chamberlain, Eagle, Churchill Lake—we fight the north wind. Much of the time, we lose. For hours it stops us—blows so hard that we can't move. It brings frustration and fans dissension. It's a real muzzler, a nose-ender. Henri's advertised philosophy—"Take it easy, see some wildlife"—has long since shrivelled, and now blows completely away. Nothing can distract him—neither a mink nor a marten nor a buff-colored hawk clinging to a swaying fir—from his apparent need not to take it easy. When the wind defeats us and we have to wait, he prowls, fidgets, and swears. At home, he can carve for ten straight hours, but here he cannot sit still.

Even Mud Pond, which is only one mile by two, is a brownish froth, uncrossable, and to get to the other side we have to make a high circle in the lee of the northern shore. Henri, whose talents do not include map reading, wanders up the inlet stream. The Blanchettes call him back. The outlet stream is too shallow for riding, so we walk down it with our hands on the floating canoes. We enter a bay of Chamberlain Lake. The bay is small—only two or three hundred acres—and almost completely landlocked. At the far end is a gap in the trees, be-yond which is open water. It is fairly hard work just to traverse this little bay, for the oncoming waves are high enough to wash into the canoes—into Henri's in particular. Finally, we near the gap, and through it can more clearly see the main body of the lake—storied, wind-ridden Chamberlain. For thirty-odd years, I have been hearing tales of this lake and how it is a whistling groove whose waves stand up like the teeth of a saw. The lake surface out there now is as white as a fast rapid. The waves are two feet high. We pause in the narrows, watch the big rollers, and take out on the shore beside them. The sun is falling. We will wait for morning and hope for calm.

Warren and I jump into the water and—to get the grit of travel out of our hair—shampoo with Lava soap. Henri un-loads his canoe and takes Mike Blanchette in his bow, and they go out to play with the big waves. The canoe nearly bron-cos them into the water, and they run for shore. Clean, feel-ing good, Warren and I build a bonfire of dry-ki in the lee of the forest and beside a big rock on the beach. Henri and the Blanchettes make their fire back in the woods. I go down in my pack for my pharmaceutical bottles, which are white and plastic and contain bourbon and gin. Henri makes himself a gin-and-Tang. There are worse things in life than stopping early for the day, surveying whitecapped water across the rim of a tin cup, standing in a wind where no-see-um no fly. War-ren and I cook dried hamburgers in a bucket of noodles. Henri eats his green jerky and gray oatmeal. Facing the big dry-ki fire, a trayful of gingerbread rises to unprecedented heights in my reflector oven. Henri wolfs it when the tray is passed to him. He announces that he has decided to buy a reflector oven.

Some years ago, with his college roommate, Henri went camping in chill weather. He had an old, thinned-out sleeping bag, in which he nearly froze, while his roommate slept comfortably in a down bag. Henri is frugal, and he generally gets along on things he makes or adapts, but when he does decide to buy he invariably seeks out things extraordinarily good of their kind. After that trip, he bought himself an Eddie Bauer down bag—a Cadillac with feathers in it. He still has it, and has kept it in excellent condition. "I hate to even mention what I used to bring into the woods, I was so ill-equipped," he says. Before he discovered pack baskets, he used plastic garbage bags. They developed holes, and water soaked his gear. He has encased his pack baskets in waterproofed canvas. As a raincoat, he still uses a plastic garbage bag with holes cut in it for his arms and head. He paid seventy-five dollars for his Hudson's Bay jacket, though. He has bought a color-television set for his shop. His stereo equipment is of an expensive order. And when his work presses in on him and he has to get away from it, he will bolt out of town sometimes on his new ten-speed Schwinn Le Tour.

At five-thirty in the morning, Henri is up and ready to go. He wants to move while the lake is relatively calm, to be ahead of the wind. There are scattered whitecaps even now. The Indians called Chamberlain Apmoojenegamook, and no one could argue with that description. If the human race has one common denominator, it is hatred of head winds, and the Indian assessment seems to have been that no one of sound mind would counterattack the winds of this long, finger-shaped lake, so they called it "Lake That Is Crossed." Apmoojenegamook: get across it and away from it as quickly as possible; used as a thoroughfare, it is too dangerous and, moreover, too much work. We move north against the morning wind, intending to make the crossing where the lake is narrowest, reducing the risk if the wind should rise. But the going is slow, and we cover less than two miles in an hour. The wind has already grown

The Survival of the Bark Canoe

considerably when we reach the narrows, where almost a mile separates the shores. What lies between them looks like broken glass.

There are two choices. On the opposite shore is a stream that leads to Eagle Lake. We can wait out the wind, and when it dies cross to the stream. Or, staying close to shore, we can continue against the wind all the way to the north end of Chamberlain, where, according to the topographic map, there is a portage that also leads to Eagle. Henri does not hesitate. We push on to the north.

The waves are just as high close in as they are in the center of the lake, but we are safer near shore, and where points of land protrude there is respite in the lee. Neither one of these canoes is very good in heavy wind. They do not hold course easily. Henri's takes in appalling amounts of water. With our drinking cups, we continually bail. Bailing is not altogether sufficient to keep Henri's canoe afloat, and twice he has to go ashore to empty it completely. His canoe was just not designed for a lake like Chamberlain. The three-inch freeboard and the ten-and-a-half-inch depth at the center thwart are inadequate dimensions for big lake waves. Moreover, the holes through which the root lashings pass—holes made in the bark below the gunwales—are less than two inches above the waterline when the canoe is loaded, and every wave that rolls by sends a bit of water through these holes. When Henri notices this, he goes into a long, revolutionary harangue about root lashings in bark canoes. If the canoes had nails in them, he says, the holes would not be there to take in the water. The only reason he does root lashings is that they look good, he says ruefully. He turns on his art. He says he wishes he had used nails. He will recover.

A wave slops over his knees. He bails. He curses the wind and praises nails. The wind is now coming down the lake in black squalls. "What a bummer!" he shouts, finally, above the wind. "What a God-damned bummer! That's all! I'm not going any farther!"

In shallow water, we get out of the canoes, steady them, and pass the gear ashore. We spread our clothes to dry, and sit in the sun. Mike discovers a leech on his ankle and pulls it away, and, stranded on a warm rock, it dies. We build a fire. We bake coffee cake, cook Cream of Wheat, and make tea. I open Thoreau and read, "A wave will gently creep up the side of the canoe and fill your lap, like a monster deliberately covering you with its slime before it swallows you, or it will strike the canoe violently and break into it. The same thing may happen when the wind rises suddenly, though it were perfectly calm and smooth there a few minutes before; so that nothing can save you, unless you can swim ashore, for it is impossible to get into a canoe again when it is upset. . . . We rarely crossed even a bay directly, from point to point, when there was wind, but made a slight curve corresponding somewhat to the shore, that we might the sooner reach it if the wind increased."

In six hours we have travelled five miles, and the wind—under the noon sun—has risen even more since we stopped. There is something cyclical but unpredictable about the rise and fall of lake winds. They decline in force, and decline a little more, and soon the water seems negotiable. So we collect our gear and start to load up. Then, like a siren, the wind goes high. We settle back. Watch the lake. The wind subsides. Again we load the canoes—only to be pushed ashore by a heavy squall.

On this same lake where we have been trying to paddle canoes with a loaded weight of several hundred pounds into heavy winds, log drivers a century ago were—by hand—moving booms that weighed many thousands of tons. They fought such winds for days and nights. They could not stop to sleep, or the wind would shove the boom backward, possibly break-

---

ing it open against the rocky shore and hopelessly scattering the logs. The boom was a teardrop enclosure of floating timber, its periphery a set of logs joined together. The boom was attached to a log raft. In a batteau (a modified dory), a three-hundred-pound anchor was carried roughly a thousand feet ahead of the raft and dropped into the lake. On the raft was a capstan, which had been made from a segment of log, with capstan bars protruding like the stubs of branches. Men on the raft strained against the capstan bars and, trudging in a circle, slowly spooled in a thousand feet of rope. Then they stood around gasping while the anchor was pulled up and taken forward another thousand feet. Even into the wind, the big boom had enough momentum to keep moving while the anchor went out again. Then the raft crew returned to the capstan bars, and the boom continued toward Bangor, at a sixth of a mile an hour.

Out of the lakes and down the Penobscot, boom crews and rivermen drove two hundred million board feet of lumber a year. They wore red shirts and caulked boots, and stepped from log to log carrying peaveys, pickpoles, pickaroons. The logs averaged sixteen feet, and those of greatest girth—the first-cut logs from the giant pines—were too big for the float down the river and were left in the forest to rot. By damming the Allagash lakes and raising them a scant twenty feet, the loggers in 1842 spilled some Allagash water into the Penobscot watershed through the Telos Cut, near the foot of Chamberlain, and timber that might have had to go to Canada could now go to the sawmills of Bangor. Down the river in spring ran waters of frightening weight—in rapids, through gorges, over falls—and in the fast water the logs ran free. Sometimes they jammed—thousands in crisscross, plugging the river. Up front, at the focus of pressure, were certain key logs. To pick them free was to "pick the jam" and send the tumult on its way. The river drivers now and then worked from boats, but more often from the banks, on foot. A wing jam was tough to pick. To pick a middle jam was sometimes fatal. If these men had been shooting each other instead of shooting rapids, their light would now shine with the cowboys'. "Go down and pick a jam on the Heater," their boss would tell them, and without a quiver they went off to die. When they attempted rescues, they enhanced the art of suicide. "Drown ten men to save two" was the accepted code of the river. They were white and Indian, and the whites on the whole were wilder—more coarse —than the Indians. Those who believed in God for the most part respected Him, but of Noah they were outspokenly critical. They thought his ark had been "a Jim Dickey house," because Noah used too much pitch.

Fortunately, the log drivers had a chronicler—a magazine writer, naturalist, and free-lance historian, whose name was Fannie Hardy Eckstorm. Her father was a Maine fur trader, and she grew up in the presence of the rivermen. She idolized them, saw them as heroes of grand dimension. She sold stories about them to the *Atlantic Monthly*, and in 1904 published the *Atlantic* stories and other pieces on the subject in a collection called *The Penobscot Man*. "It has always been the glory of the West Branch Drive that it had so many such men, every one of whom placed the welfare of those logs above his own life," she wrote. They were "supple young foam-walkers," in her eyes, and they could "traverse the froth of those white rapids without wetting a shoe-tap." Upriver they went—as many as two hundred of them—to start the drive with the spring high water, and, come what may, it was a matter of pride to have the logs in Bangor by the end of June. For two months, they ate "sow-belly an' Y.E.B.'s" (pork and yellow-eyed beans), and they drank themselves to heaven on the Fourth of July.

Joe Aitteon worked the West Branch Drive. He was only twenty-four when, in September 1853, he made his trip with

---

Thoreau. In his thirties, he was elected governor of his tribe, and in 1870, aged forty-one, he died on the drive. Paddle in hand, he drowned in the Heater, where the water ran so white, the river drivers said, "a brick would swim." In command of a full batteau crew, a mixture of whites and Indians, he had been sent to pick a jam, and the boat was staved in and swamped and carried on into even heavier rapids. Aitteon was a swimmer, and by leaving the boat he might have survived —as did others, including Dingbat Prouty. Aitteon, however, died with the nonswimmers, whom he was trying to save. Far below the rapids was a calm, still stretch of the river, and a crew of drivers working the banks there suddenly saw a long stern paddle—unmistakably Aitteon's, with its blue blade and its carved eagle—rise vertically halfway out of the water.

It was Eckstorm's opinion that Thoreau was "lacking in penetration" and had "failed to get the measure" of Aitteon. Thoreau had missed a chance to sketch a character of considerable worldliness and with a gift for leadership—never mind that Aitteon was young when Thoreau knew him. "Thoreau hired an Indian to be aboriginal," she explained, and he tended to ignore anything that did not accord with his preconceptions. Aitteon said "By George!" too much when he should have been talking pidgin. His true character failed to emerge in *The Maine Woods*. Thoreau had a "luckless knack of blundering," according to Eckstorm, and "when he came in contact with men, in his own phrase, 'he improved his opportunity to be ignorant.' " He was, after all, the "hermit of Walden," she said. He was "naïve," and he could not grasp a "truly strange" and "subtle matter" when one was brought to his attention. For example, a mysterious death had taken place at a riverine landmark called the Gray Rock of Abol, and Joe Polis, Thoreau's other Indian guide, tried to tell him the story. Thoreau deflected the conversation before Polis could get to the point, and thus Thoreau, in Eckstorm's words, "bungled utterly" what she called "the most significant incident that ever came under his observation while he was in the Maine woods." Fortunately, though, the Indian had told at least a fragment of the story to this "man who wrote everything down, even the things he did not understand," and, equipped with Thoreau's thin clue, Eckstorm herself went to the rivermen and uncovered the full, long tale. The gray rock is flat and stands in quiet water. Reduced to essentials, the story concerned a log driver who suddenly disappeared from the rock, never again to be seen alive. The day was clear. He was not killed by man or nature. He died because he was in the act of cursing God:

> The man who had seen this told the others. "I seen him stand there like he was on a barn floor, and I seen him lift up his fist an' shake it right stret in the face of old Katahdin, an' I hearn him holler like his voice would rattle lead inside him, 'To hell with God!' An' then when I looked the Gray Rock was all empty, an' in the water I seen only his two sets of fingers movin' slow-like in the mist that sticks close to the black slick of the falls. I seen 'em open once, an' then they shut an' was gone."
> "That was a judgment," said the men one to another.

It never occurred to Eckstorm to question what she saw as the high purpose of the West Branch Drive. Moving those logs downstream was pure epic to her, and the goal—beyond challenge—was the common good. One suspects, therefore, that Thoreau annoyed her less by what he failed to say than by what he said most strongly. One imagines her reaching for a pickpole when, in *The Maine Woods*, she came upon this:

> The reader will perceive that the result of this particular

damming about Chamberlain Lake is, that the head-waters of the St. John are made to flow by Bangor . . . thus turning the forces of nature against herself, that they might float their spoils out of the country. . . . The wilderness experiences a sudden rise of all her streams and lakes, she feels ten thousand vermin gnawing at the base of her noblest trees. . . . The chopper . . . speaks of a "berth" of timber, a good place for him to get into, just as a worm might. When the chopper would praise a pine, he will commonly tell you that the one he cut was so big that a yoke of oxen stood on its stump; as if that were what the pine had grown for, to become the footstool of oxen.

Henri Vaillancourt's great-great-grandfather was a river driver, and he drowned on the job.

Well beyond noon, we are still held fast by the wind. It has subsided a little, but the lake remains a whitecapped sea. One senses that we will be on it soon. Henri is using the word "bummer" at about double the rate he was using it an hour or two ago. The wind and Henri's patience are drawing lines across the day, and when the lines converge we will load up and go.

Just a few feet inside the treeline on the shore, the wind is filtered and calmed. Looking out on the lake from between two trees is like looking through a window at a storm. It is pleasant here, and warm. I could stay here for a week, not to mention the hours that are left in this day. I would very much like to sleep and read and—no matter how much time it takes —outlast the wind. But that would be the Indians' way, and Henri is not an Indian. Restless, impatient to move forward and cover ground, he paws the beach. He throws a rock in the water. He curses the wind. He says, "Christ, it's quiet enough. Let's go." It would take a meteorologist to tell us whether the wind is stronger or weaker than it was when we put in to shore. The waves are rolling hard, but the waiting, apparently, has built the case for going. We load the canoes and shove off.

We dig into the lake. We paddle and bail, bail and paddle —draining the bilge with drinking cups. We are struggling to get to the north end, about three miles away, and gambling that the wind will not rise to an even higher level before we are in the lee of the north-end woods. Why do we need these miles now? Why does Henri have this compulsion to move? Is he Patton? Sherman? Hannibal? How *could* he be, when the only regimentation he can tolerate is the kind he creates as he goes along? These are thoughts not composed in tranquillity but driven into the mind by the frontal wind. Why do we defer to him? Why do we look to his decisions? Is it only because he made the canoes, because the assumption is that he knows what is best for them and knows what they can do and ought not to do? His judgment draws attention to itself, right enough. On the Penobscot River, he went "out for a spin" in heavy, gray dusk and was gone long after dark— much longer than he wished or intended. What was he doing? He was struggling to pick his way through boulders and up a set of minor rapids he could not see. A camper on the river-bank, that same day, asked him if his canoe was not too low in the freeboard for paddling on open lakes, and he said, "Not really. They don't really ride low. You can design a canoe to do anything." But here he is on Chamberlain Lake, bailing six inches of water from between his knees and whisking with his paddle, while Warren, like a tractor, pulls the canoe. A suspicion that has been growing comes out in the wind: Henri's expertise stops in "the yard"; out here he is as green as his jerky.

After two hours of paddling, we have gone a mile and three-quarters, but we are at least not going backward. We begin to feel the protection of the land ahead of us, and Rick and I point off the wind and head more directly for the carry at the northeast corner of the lake. Mike, though, does not like rolling in the troughs of the waves. He says to his older brother,

"Do you think we'll have trouble taking these waves broadside, Rick?"

"We'll head out a little," Rick answers.

"No. Follow Henri, Rick. Follow Henri."

Mike is a pessimistic soul, and he is convinced that—as he puts it—"if the canoe turns over, you're a goner." All the more touching is his belief that Henri will see him through.

Rick defers to Henri, too, but less so. Rick is Henri's lifelong friend. The differences between them must attract the one to the other. Rick is self-effacing and thoughtful, and he is less impressed than he might be with his own intelligence. He has no apparent special talent, and he admires greatly Henri's single-minded dedication, his artistry, and his adroitness with his tools. Rick introduced Henri to Beethoven and, in all likelihood, to Thoreau. Subtly, in one way or another, he seems to have been helping Henri along for years. Rick seems to sense frailty and unsureness under Henri's carapace of bluntness, and is always ready to give him the benefit of the doubt. Rick is sensitive to Henri's insensitivities—to his opinionated arrogance, to his inconsiderate manner, to his platoon-leading orders. In Rick's long, contemplative glances, Warren and I can see him weighing the effect of Henri's directives.

Warren, who has the misfortune to be paddling in Henri's bow, is by now suffering from acute propinquity, and, being a silent man, takes it out on the lake. His strokes are delivered with killing strength, and in their canoe it is Warren who is defeating the wind. The more Henri orders him around, the harder Warren must work to work off his anger. It is an asset to have such an engine in the bow. Warren and I are more or less guests on this trip, so we defer to Henri. We have, however, tried to make suggestions—where to stay, when to go, what to head for—but the results have been dismal, and we have learned that suggestions are challenges to the tacit commander. We go when he is ready. We stop when he wants to stop. We stay where he wants to stay. He does not seek out the consensus of the group, and when it comes his way he almost automatically rejects it.

Some of these thoughts subside with the wind as we move in among the sedges in the corner of the lake. We are finished at least with the winds of Chamberlain, having climbed ten miles through them an inch at a time.

An isthmus half a mile wide separates Chamberlain from Eagle, and a steam-powered continuous cable once ran across it, hauling logs from one lake to the other on little steel trucks. All the thousands of bolts, steel clamps, steel saddle, steel tracks, and fourteen tons of cable were brought into the woods over winter ice or in canoes and other boats, following the route we have followed. The conveyor lasted about six years— at the beginning of the twentieth century. Beside what is left of it we portage now. The track is still there, upgrown with trees. The portage trail is firm and open, and easy going all the way. Just before the shore of Eagle, we drop our packs, set down the canoes, and stare in disbelief at what may be the most incongruous sight any of us has ever seen: two full-scale steam locomotives, alone in the woods, abandoned. They, too, were brought in here in fragments and assembled in the woods. Standard-gauge track—seventy-five miles from the nearest railroad—was laid so that logs could be moved a few miles over the height of land. The trains began running in 1927 and were used for only a season or two. The track they ran on has been all but closed over by the woods.

We go down to the shore and look at Eagle Lake. It is a big one, and four miles of it stretch north in front of us before it bends to the west and out of sight. The wind and the white-caps are worse than they were on Chamberlain—a forbidding gale. Henri sucks on a blade of grass and paces around saying, "Christ, what a bummer." It is as clear to him as to the rest of us that there will be no moving into such a wind. We eat lunch. It is four-thirty in the afternoon. The wind will drop soon, Henri tells us. Meanwhile, Henri's packs are still at the other end of the carry. The Blanchettes go back to fetch them for him.

After two more hours, big gray waves are still coming down the lake, rolling before the wind. Unfortunately, this is a bad place to spend a night, because the mechanized loggers gave it a century's fouling and the century isn't over yet. Rust is everywhere—rusty spikes, rusty hunks of the conveyor. To accommodate incoming logs, landfill was shoved into the lake, so the shore is artificial and swampy and strewn with boulders and still jagged with the corpses of water-killed trees. Mike wants to stay here, in this oxidized hole of commerce. He is so tired that it looks good to his eyes. He says it is as good as any campsite we've seen. Rick watches Henri and says nothing. Warren and I move our packs up the portage trail, planning to sleep there and avoid the junk yard. When we return to the lakeshore, Henri says the wind is declining. It is seven-thirty now, and the lake is indeed calming down. We will paddle at night, Henri says, and take advantage of the absence of the wind. Warren looks around with incredulity, and even apprehension, in his eyes. He appears to be wondering how to make a straitjacket. We got up at five today. We have paddled ten miles into blistering wind and followed that with a portage. Now we are told that we are going to set out on another big lake for God knows where in the dark of night. Under the influence of the wind, our affection for our leader has been waning all day, and it now levels out at zero. We turn without comment and walk away.

Warren, who was recently discharged from the Marine Corps, says, "I feel as if I were back in uniform." We go up the trail to our packs and our tent, and pick them up, and

The Survival of the Bark Canoe

carry them back to the lake. It is Henri's trip. We will paddle tonight.

There is a cut, a sluiceway, a small canal, that penetrates the shore. It was used to float logs to the conveyor. Henri and Warren load their canoe in the sluiceway and push off toward the open lake. Rick and Mike and I fill our canoe, and while we are handling the packs a six-inch leech excitedly swims among us, trying to get in on the fun. With everything aboard, the three of us prepare to step in. We do not know that two iron spikes, set in timber, stand upright underwater, the tip of each less than an inch from the underside of the floating canoe. We step in, one at a time, and we give the canoe a shove. It does not move. Water spurts upward in fountains, fast enough to swamp us instantly.

Jumping out, we shout for Henri. We unload the canoe, lift it ashore, and roll it over. Rick is struggling to control his distress. His canoe, a treasure to him, has two ugly holes in it, large enough and ragged enough to make one wonder how it can continue the trip. Henri, examining the wounds, curses Rick for negligence, for irresponsibility, for failure as custodian of a bark canoe. Rick does not try to demur.

Now, all at once, Henri stops his harangue and changes utterly. The man who has been pouting, sucking grass, and cursing the wind all afternoon is suddenly someone else—is now, in a sense, back in his yard, his hands on a torn canoe. The lacerations are broad, and the bark around them is in flaps with separating layers. "Make a fire," he says, and Warren and I move off for wood. "Rick, Mike, get bark. Get strips of bark. And cut a green stick."

Henri goes down into his pack for the small paper bag in which he keeps his pot of pitch. He has been touching up the canoes from time to time since we started, and now has about six ounces left.

The fire is going. He sets the pot on two burning sticks. It seems so vulnerable. What if the pitch spills or blazes up? Where are we then, with one canoe?

Thirty minutes ago, we were standing apart in groups, tense to the edges of rage, some of us committing verbal mutiny. Now we are all bustling in service to Henri—his surgical nurses, offering instruments to his hand. First—with his crooked knife—he cuts away what appears to me to be a considerable amount of bark, trimming the split and flapping laminations. He does not cut all the way through, for with the exception of the actual punctures most of the damage is in the outer layers. He cuts a wide, shallow crater around each wound—four to five inches in diameter—taking away about half the bark's layers.

He asks for the green stick and the fresh bark, and with them he makes a torch. He lights it, and moves it close to the bottom of the canoe. He takes a deep breath and steadily blows flame into and around one of the punctures. Gradually, the bark there lightens in tone and becomes bone-dry. Henri says it is not impatience but necessity that causes him to use the torch. Even if he were to wait many hours, the rent bark would not completely dry; and "if bark is not absolutely dry the pitch won't stick."

It is now too dark for him to see. He calls for the flashlight, and I get it from my pack and shine it on the canoe as he works. He removes the pot from the fire and—with a flat stick—paints the entire damaged area with pitch while the Blanchettes, one at each end, hold the canoe level. Henri pulls out the tail of his shirt and cuts it off. It is broadcloth, and he cuts out of it a circular piece, which he presses down onto the pitch. Calling for the pot again, he paints on more pitch, until the cloth is completely covered. Then, as the pitch cools, he presses it repeatedly with his thumb, licking his thumb as he goes along to keep it from sticking. The finished patch is a black circle, about six inches in diameter. It is in the center of the bottom of the canoe. "At home I'll cut an eye of bark and put a rim around it," Henri says. "Then the patch, you know, will look better."

It is too late to move now. We sleep beside the canoes and get up at five-thirty to continue the repair. The pitch, heating up in the morning fire, bursts into flame. Henri runs to it and smothers it with a coffeepot lid, but some is lost. Minutes later, the pitch catches fire again.

"Our pitch after this is going to be nil," Henri says. "That's no problem, though. I should have brought more pitch, but we can always get spruce gum. There's plenty of it around here."

Applying what is left to the other rip in the canoe, he says casually, "I've never had this happen before. I've never had to patch a canoe before." He pauses, and licks his thumb. "You could break a whole end off in the woods and still fix the canoe—that is, if you'd built a canoe before," he says. "If you hadn't, I think you'd be in trouble."

Mike says, "I wonder what will happen if those patches let go in the middle of the lake."

And Henri says, "I don't think they will."

The lake is flat calm—mirror condition—and the sky cloudless. It is seven-thirty. We load up and go. Early in the trip, we tied almost nothing to the canoes, but now every pack is secured with thongs, ropes, and strings. Our boots are tied to the thwarts, since we launch and paddle without them.

The canoe is dry, and sound, and it seems to slide on oil. It cuts an arrow of a wake directly north across the open water— four, five miles—with an ease that launches jokes again, canoe to canoe.

"So. How are you?"

"And how are your wife and camels?"

Now, though, in the last half mile before the end of Eagle, a cruising loon leans forward and gives its long, lamentful cry. When, on a dead-calm day, a loon breaks a silence with such a cry, it is almost invariably a signal that a wind—not a breeze but a sudden, heavy wind—is coming. A minute passes. Two. There is no sign of it. Three. Four. On the last stretch of lake before us, the surface suddenly appears scratched, like rubber prepared for a patch. Moments later, a stiff wind ruffles our

The Survival of the Bark Canoe

shirts. It is not a puff but a steady push. Waves rise quickly, and minutes later they are capped white.

"Mother."

"God."

"Damn."

"Bitch."

We have to fight to finish the lake.

Fortunately, narrow waters lead on to the north for three miles—dam-drowned stretches, actually, of the Allagash River. The riparian forests temper the wind somewhat, but still it comes at us hard down the alley.

"What a—"

"Bummer."

Long before we reach and slide through them, the wind brings the sweet scent of a rich purple grove of pickerelweed.

Henri has begun to bail with exceptional vigor. His canoe is showing trouble—taking in more water than before. The land widens again to either side, and we move onto Churchill Lake, where the waves are as high and the wind as strong as they were at any time on Chamberlain. The lake inclines to the northeast, and the wind is quartering on us now. A thousand yards out, Henri turns to face it. He cannot take even the small amount of extra water that comes with quartering waves. His canoe is filling up. Racing a serious leak, he and Warren cut straight through the wind. Ahead of them is a strip of sand-and-pebble beach. Bailing as they go, they make it. We are two and a half hours, and nine miles, from breakfast—not bad against a rising head wind and with another sick canoe.

We eat an early lunch—Rick, Warren, Mike, and I—and lie on the beach and take the sun, and watch Henri fix the canoe. He is collected and professional. He does not rail at his canoes as he rails at the wind. His problem now is no less serious than the one after the accident last night, and in the repair the degree of difficulty appears to be, if anything, greater.

A longitudinal seam connecting two pieces of bark below the waterline has broken its sewing, and a gap has opened. When he made the canoe, he sewed that area too close to the edge of the bark, and the root stitching has now broken through to the edge. It is a wonder the canoe did not founder.

Henri's confidence is undisturbed, and he goes into the forest for a fresh root. He digs a spruce root—five or six feet, which is more than he needs—and returns to the beach. With his crooked knife he rubs the bark off the root until it looks, and wriggles, like a cord of white rubber. (Indians used roots for fishing lines.) He bites one end, splitting it, and then—with a shaking, shivery manipulation—pulls the root into halves from one end to the other. The splitting, as it goes along, will tend to favor one side. The idea is to sense which way it wants to go and to correct the split in favor of the other side. A novice could dig up roots by the dozen and not split one successfully, but Henri refuses to be praised for his swift execution of the trick. "There's nothing to it," he says. "You get the knack quickly. You feel them going one way or the other and you just correct it." Around Greenville, he has found white-pine roots twenty-five feet long. Like the roots of the black spruce, they run close to the surface and are easy to collect. White spruce will not do. Joe Polis once said of the roots of white spruce, "No good, break, can't split 'em." And they run too deep in the ground.

Henri takes a close look at the position of the break in the seam and is pleased to find that it is directly under a rib. "Good," he says. "The repair won't show." And he taps the rib aside. His awls are at home, but he has picked up a nail somewhere, and he uses it now to bore holes through the planking and the bark. The root is soon moving through the planking and out through the bark and back again in a set of cobbler's stitches—Henri reaching around the canoe, hugging it, to draw the sewing tight. He is sewing not only bark to bark

The Survival of the Bark Canoe

(near the original seam) but also bark to planking, to give the repair increased authority. When the sewing is finished and tied off, bright sutures mar the planking, but Henri taps the rib back in, and—as he said it would—it completely hides the job.

Warren, sitting up on one elbow, tugs his beard, looks at me, and says, "I have a question. What in the name of hell would we ever do without him?"

We are about as far north as we are going to go. On Thoreau's canoe trips in the Maine woods, his most northern campsite was on Pillsbury Island, in Eagle Lake. "We did not intend to go far down the Allegash," he wrote in his journal, "but merely to get a view of the great lakes which are its source." Henri may have taken his cue from this, for his own intention has been much the same: to scour the scenes of the big Allagash lakes and then to bend off in another direction and go upstream to the highest sources of the river—and to Allagash Lake itself, the best and remotest of them all.

To the north, meanwhile, we have some five more miles to paddle—to Churchill Dam, which raised the water here enough to boom logs, there to see (but not to shoot) the Chase Rapids of the Allagash River. We shove off and round a point and buck the head wind all the way. Henri's canoe is as good as ever; that is to say, it takes in the usual amount of wave lap but nothing through the re-sewn seam.

There is a Maine state ranger station at Churchill Dam. The ranger comes out and looks in wonder at the two birchbark canoes. He is short and dark, with a creased face and a quick smile. He says that he has seen thousands of canoes in his time on the Allagash Wilderness Waterway but none, ever, like these. The canoes are exquisite, he agrees. Those paddles, though, those little Indian paddles—"now, they would drive you foolish." He, in his turn, has something to show—three fresh bullet holes in his cabin door, through which, last night, he fired three fresh bullets at bears that were crowding his porch trying to claw their way in.

In broad bends of white water, the Allagash River flows away from the dam and the cabin. The rapids, continuous for several miles, are not heavy but are broad, shallow, and rocky. Henri says if he were going on downriver he would portage around them.

I ask him why.

"The canoes would be all right," he says. "I'd trust them. I just wouldn't trust myself. I've never been in rapids before."

The ranger controls the river. Each evening around five, he says, when people downriver are presumably camped for the night, he closes the gates—turns off the water. Suddenly, the Chase Rapids are no longer white or rapid. They become a set of island pools, as does the rest of the river. In the morning at six, before the campers are up, the ranger opens the gates. The river fills while the campers are cooking breakfast. When they are ready to shove off, there is water to float them. We ourselves shove off—heading back, for the time being, in the direction from which we have come.

For a while, we sail down Churchill Lake, pleased to have foxed the wind, but the wind, the anthropomorphic wind, will not be so tricked and cheated. It quickly dies behind the sail —dies as fast as it rose in the morning—and leaves us to paddle under the glare of the sun. Three, four, five hours we paddle, until the sun is almost down. The rate of jokes flying between the canoes declines steadily with the lengthening of the afternoon. We hint, suggest, urge, and ultimately beg Henri to stop for the day, which he does, with good grace, at sundown. Even with the time spent patching and sewing two disabled canoes, we have paddled twenty-five miles since we slept. There is an ice-cold spring in the woods near the campsite. The spring water gives altitude to gin in a way that the tepid water of these shallow lakes can never do. Even before the stars are bright, we are half asleep. The canoes are over-turned by the shore. I remember that books say never to leave canoes overturned in bear country, because a bear wondering what's inside may smash its way in. Too late, too tired, to worry about bears. Warren snores through the night like a bear—a bass to the treble of the loons.

Allagash Stream, the highest reach of the river, drops to the head of Chamberlain Lake from the west-northwest. Recrossing the isthmus carry, we go in the morning to the mouth of the stream. By noon, we are literally in the water. As it pours toward us, it is too shallow to be paddled, too shallow to be poled. There is nothing to do but frog it—get out of the canoes and walk them up the current. If it is this shallow here, it is not in all likelihood going to get any deeper as we go along; therefore, as the map informs us, the best we can hope for is a seven-mile walk in the water.

Alternative routes are, for various reasons, less attractive, and do not include Allagash Lake, whose remoteness is written in its approaches: from the east, seven miles' sloshing up a rocky stream; from the west, a portage of three miles, by far the longest in the Allagash woods. So we drag the canoes—in two, three inches of water, jumping, bubbling, rushing at us. We lift them at the gunwales to reduce the draw. Now and again, we slide and fall on rock shelves covered with algae. In pools, we go in to the hips, to the chest, all the way. The cool water feels good coming on. It feels good rushing around the

The Survival of the Bark Canoe

ankles. It feels good closing overhead. I would prefer to frog fifty miles up a forest stream than paddle ten against a big lake head wind.

Often, it is necessary to heave rocks aside to create a channel wide enough for the canoes. On many of the rocks are heavy streaks of paint or aluminum left by hundreds of canoes that have come banging down this river in varying levels of water under the care of people who did not give a damn what they hit. What comes home once more at the sight of those aluminum-covered rocks is the world of difference in the way we feel toward our canoes, and it is the central pleasure of this trip: we care so much about them. We scrape a little, too, and it can't be helped. *Tant pis*, as Henri says. Bark leaves no marks behind. Warren, leading, voraciously sculpts the river —kicking stones aside, lifting rocks so large they appear to be ledges and stuffing them into the banks. Then he hauls the canoe up the freeways he has made. Henri walks behind with a rope in his hand. It is tied to the stern, which he moves from side to side, as if the canoe were a horse on a halter.

The stream is a white-water primer, for it is flowing much like a riverine rapid, which is what it is, scaled down. All in miniature, the haystacks, the standing waves, the souse holes, the eddies, the satin-water pillows are here, and usually there is a place to go—a *fil d'eau*—that is deeper and better than anywhere else. One learns to read the stream. After four hours, we have gone two miles.

Henri remarks that he is now hungry enough to eat a moose, and wouldn't mind trying if one were to appear.

"You have to see one before you can eat one, Henri."

"And how are your wife and your cattle?"

"God bless you, well."

A windfall fir lies across the stream now and stops us altogether, but Henri unsheathes his axe and sends flotillas of chips down the current. The log drops into the water. We

shove it out of the way. The air is chill. The sky, all but un-
noticed by us, has clouded over, and the afternoon is almost
gone. Even Henri is ready to stop. The map shows a waterfall
ahead, a place to camp beside it. I see a clam, pick it up, and
toss it into the canoe—another, another, beds of them in
the eddies of the stream. I remember a time when I was hungry on the Susquehanna River and hunted it for miles for
freshwater clams, peering down over the side of a canoe, finding nothing but an empty shell. These clams of the Allagash
are squirting, vigorous, living, lovely freshwater clams. Warren
and I have been eating freeze-dried food, which I, having
had little of it before, was interested in trying; and, having
tried it days on end, I look forward all the more to the clams.

"Why are you picking those things up?" Henri wants to
know.

"We're going to eat them. Do you want some?"

"Not really."

Glances are exchanged between Vaillancourt and the
Blanchettes. Madness will out, and they are sure they have
seen it now.

Others have preceded us to Little Allagash Falls—a man in
his twenties, his wife, their malamute puppy, and their twenty-
foot wood-and-canvas Old Town canoe. It is new, green, un-
deniably beautiful. Twenty feet is a lot of canoe, and the hull
has many fresh scratches, despite his care. He is in the wilderness business, he says, with an outfitting shop and a dealership
in canoes—an interest that developed in his boyhood, when
he made long canoe trips with Keewaydin in Canada in terrain where portages sometimes did not exist and had to be
scouted and cut. Where on earth, he wonders, did we get those
canoes?

"I make them."

"You *make* them?"

"Full time," Henri says, his eyes averted toward the falls.

The Survival of the Bark Canoe

"May I photograph them?"

"Oh, sure."

We carry around the falls and pitch our tents near the upstream side, before it begins to rain. It rains hard. Henri brings up one of the canoes and turns it over near the fire and runs his tarp from the canoe to a pair of trees. The shelter gives some protection to the fire and more than some to us, and we wait out the worst of the rain.

"Just a shower," I say.

"I don't know," Mike says. "I don't know" means "I disagree."

We steam the clams open in a four-quart pot, and remove them from their shells. We sprinkle them with salt and roll them in Bisquick and fry them in very hot Crisco. Henri says they are *moules frites*. "*Frites*," on his tongue, is "*frètes*."

"Clam? Have a clam?"

Everyone is hungry. The Blanchettes are hungry and Henri is hungry, but they will have no part of the clams.

The larger clams are chewy, go down with some resistance. But the smaller ones are crisp, succulent, tender, delicious, Allagash-Ipswich, golden brown.

"Clam?"

"Not really. Not yet, anyways."

"What are you waiting for—to see if we die?"

The three of them—Rick, Mike, Henri—are to varying extents wavering, but they still refuse. They eat their jerky and their boiled dinners. Warren and I alone are eating the clams. There are two left.

"I'll take one."

Out comes the hand of Henri. In all the culinary spectrum, there is not much he likes, but one great exception is clams. He has told us how he drives to favorite places to buy pints and quarts of fried clams. Now he eats this one. He eats the other.

Rain again—heavy rain. We go into the tents at half past seven, and get into our bags to sleep it away. The rain sounds good, if nothing else, and it should put more water in the stream. It comes in torrents down through the trees.

Warren outsnores the sound of the rain. Henri, too. The harder the day, the more vibrant the snore. I kick them. I pick up a loose boot and hit them. The effort is wasted.

Lake, portage, and stream, we covered only ten miles today —in twelve hours of travel. I will confess that, on the whole, I don't mind these long days. I like the purpose in the motion, the clear possession of a course to follow, the sense of journey. I like to go to sleep early and rise with the sun. In these respects, I guess, I am much like Henri.

At eleven, there is a cry from Rick Blanchette—from out of the rain and the black. He wants to know—this politest of all people—if he can come to our tent, since his tent is not functioning to the end toward which it was designed. When he arrives, the flashlight discovers that he is totally soaked. His hair is matted and dripping. His clothes are as wet as they would be if he had fallen into a lake. He shivers. His brother's long frame now comes in as well, clothes and body equally drenched. They report that their sleeping bags are soaked through, and all their personal gear. The rain pours hard as ever. It is impossible for five people to lie down in our tent except in a stack, like cordwood. So the Blanchettes sit up through the night, silently. Hours go by. They doze on their haunches, and shiver. Henri, before returning to sleep, observes with mild remonstrance in his voice that they made a mistake in bringing that tent, which has the appearance of something sent for with a hunk of a cereal box. It would have been much better, he says, to bring their other tent, no matter that it was larger and heavier. Toward five in the morning, with dawn breaking and the rain so light now it is almost mist,

The Survival of the Bark Canoe

Warren and I get up and go out, putting the Blanchettes in our bags, where they drop at once to sleep.

They sleep until eight. Warren and I meanwhile nurse up the fire and bake bread for the day. Henri, up around seven, pulls on his river-stiff leather shoes. (They are all he has, and he wears no socks.) He makes his breakfast. He then picks up a clamshell and rubs the bark off a cedar. He seems to be testing the effectiveness of the shell as a tool, and its score must be high, for he has swiftly denuded a part of the tree. Less than ten miles ahead of us, after Allagash Stream and at the far end of Allagash Lake, is the long carry. Rick, who is determined to carry his canoe himself all the way, will need something more than the paddles on his shoulders to absorb the weight. With cedar bark, Henri makes for him a tumpline. It is eight feet long and is broad and soft in the center, where it will cross his forehead. "When the canoe was lifted upon his head bottom up," wrote Thoreau, describing Polis on a carry, "a band of cedar-bark, tied to the crossbar . . . passed round his breast, and another longer one, outside of the last, round his forehead."

By nine, we are back in the stream, which must have been helped by the rain but is nonetheless shallower than it was below the falls, so the going is slower. It is necessary to stop more often to make a channel among the shelves and gravels and small cascades. Conversation is scarce and inclined to be snappish. The rain has stopped, though. The overcast is cracking, and we are more than halfway up the stream. Three more miles will kill it.

In late morning, as a kind of energizer, I eat some freeze-dried vanilla ice cream. It sticks in my teeth like white cement. As candy, it is not bad, despite its texture—tough meringue—but, no matter what its origins may have been, it is bunkum to call it ice cream. With breakfast, Warren and I had freeze-dried pears. Semi-permeable, they had soaked for hours, but the water got through only halfway, so what we ate might have been pear-covered chewing gum. Freeze-dried peaches, a day or so ago, had the consistency of garden slugs. The ecological insurrection has yielded some pyrrhic triumphs, and one of them is commercial freeze-dried food. Whose idea of wilderness travel could be embodied, enhanced, or even faintly expressed in Mountain House Freeze Dried Raspberry Apple Crunch? Mountain House Freeze Dried Tuna Salad? Rich-Moor "Astro" Freeze-Dried Eggs? Yet it moves. Moves off the shelf and into the wilderness, sold. It creates, apparently, a sense of hardtack and pemmican within a gourmet context. On a canoe trip, the weight of food is not of crucial importance. There is something to be said for the lighter weight of freeze-dried food on the trail, but not enough to justify Mountain House Freeze Dried Shrimp Creole, Mountain House Freeze Dried Beef Stroganoff, Tea Kettle Freeze Dried Turkey Tetrazzini—violations of the rites of the wild. They are expensive, these shining foil packets from the rugged boutiques. They represent a return to nature —with money. Next time out, I'm going back to beans and bacon, prunes, rice—macaroni, too. I have had enough for a lifetime of freeze-dried "chunk chicken" and freeze-dried "beef almondine." I would prefer to eat emerald jerky in peanut-butter sauce.

I appear to be the only one who likes Allagash Stream. Warren is cursing and hauling; so are the Blanchettes. Henri's vocabulary has collapsed, condensed; "bummer" is the only remaining word. We have covered three miles in five hours, but the sun is warm, and ahead is a break in the trees. The trip up the Rat, in the Northwest Territories, involves nine days of this—hauling canoes a foot at a time into oncoming water that is not merely cool, as it is here, but ice-cold, pouring from Arctic mountains. The yield is a remote and beauti-

The Survival of the Bark Canoe

ful height of land among the mountains, then the short carry, the long run down the Pacific side. It may seem a strange way to travel, walking uphill with a canoe along as a kind of packhorse, but, given enough water to float the canoe, the experience is not disagreeable, and I wish we could all do it for those nine northern days.

The lake is close, and clams proliferate in the last bends of the stream. Henri, as he goes along, scoops them up, and so do we all, making piles of them in the canoes.

Now, after fourteen hours in the stream, a night of naps, and a soaking rain, we stand in the outlet of Allagash Lake. The most distant point we can see is perhaps four miles away —a clear shot down open water past a fleet of islands. The lake is broad in all directions, and is ringed with hills and minor mountains. Its pristine, unaltered shoreline is edged with rock —massive outcroppings, sloping into the water, interrupting the march of the forest. It is a reward, this lake—handsome, natural, serene, remote, the long stream and the long portage holding it aloof on either end.

We unload the canoes near a huge slope of rock, which has baked for some hours in steady sun. Tents, sleeping bags, clothes, shoes—everything we have is soon spread out there like wash on a Spanish hillside. We swim with soap and then spread ourselves out, too. The heat in the rocks rises into the bones and drifts us into sleep. An hour dries it all. Even the Blanchettes' sodden sleeping bags are dry and warm and light as fluff.

Out on the lake is the glint of a metal canoe. It approaches unsteadily. The paddlers ask for Allagash Stream. They wear bathing suits, and their bellies are pale and fat. They appear to have stepped out of an airplane and into the canoe. Unbelievably, that is exactly what they have done. A float plane has set them down with their canoe on a pond near a corner of the lake, and they have come down a stream from there. What a travesty! What a majestic bummer! It is the law of the state that no plane can land in this lake, an airplane being an affront to the Allagash Wilderness Waterway. At least, no airplane is going to help these two drag seven miles downstream to Chamberlain. More aluminum for the rocks.

Naturally, the wind has risen, for we have come into its purview again. No doubt because we are heading southwest, the wind is coming from that direction. We load and go. It is three in the afternoon. The wind accelerates, and the waves rise high. Now we are digging again, as hard as ever—more work than we might have hoped for. Henri informs us there is even more ahead. He wants to make the long carry today. He wants to paddle against this head wind the six miles to the end of the lake, take out the canoes, and portage three miles. Return trips included, the carry should take four hours. That would bring us to the far side—all going well—at 9 or 10 P.M. The great beauty of this lake apparently means nothing to him. He has worked for two days to get to it, and now wants to rush across it and portage away from it in the dusk and dark. He is paddling hard. He is piqued at the discord his plan evokes. Sentiment against it runs four to one.

The benevolent wind attempts the rescue, blasting us so hard it is all we can do to fight to the lee of an island. Henri's canoe nearly swamps. We dash to another island, and work its lee, and another. Wind and mutiny in the end prevail. We pitch our tents beside Allagash Lake.

Henri rigs the tarp over the Blanchettes' tent, and they dig a trench around it that could divert a river. Warren and I steam open the clams. We fry them, as before, and this time Henri squats near, waiting for the clams to be done. The Blanchettes approach and wait beside him, also on their haunches, a little behind him. Onto a plate on the ground by the fire Warren tosses a clam. Henri picks it up and eats it. He praises it. Warren flips more clams onto the plate. Henri eats

The Survival of the Bark Canoe

them. The eyes of the Blanchettes follow the clams from pan to plate to Henri's mouth. But toward the plate they do not make a move. Warren and I are not particularly hungry now, and, in any case, are too absorbed with this tableau to enter it and break it. Henri is the alpha wolf. The others in the pack, no matter how hungry they may be, will watch but not budge while the alpha dines. In time, the Blanchettes do get some clams—each about an eighth of the total—and they eat them hungrily, for they are running out of food.

Henri, after dinner, carves by the campfire, working on a piece of balsam and a piece of cedar until each is a lath that seems perfectly squared. He tests for tensile strength, slowly bending each length of wood until it strains and cracks. "The cedar is all right," he says. "But this balsam is nowhere. Hang it up."

There is a time of change in a wilderness trip when patterns that have been left behind fade beneath the immediacies of wind, sun, rain, and fire, and a different sense of distance, of shelter, of food. We made that change when we were still in the Penobscot valley, and by now I, for one, would like to keep going indefinitely; the change back will bring a feeling of loss, an absence of space, a nostalgia for the woods. The end has come, though. Henri has run out of Tang. Tang is his halazone, his palate's defense, his agent conversional for pure lakes and streams. Without Tang, he is without water.

The Caucomgomoc roadhead is about twenty miles away— prospectively a long day's journey, since three of the twenty miles are forest portage trail. We are up in the morning at half past four.

On the water, in the post-dawn light, the canoes slide across a mirror so nearly perfect that the image could be inverted without loss of detail. The lake is absolutely still, and mist thickens its distances and subdues in gray its islands and circumvallate hills. Warren and Henri are perhaps a hundred feet farther out than we are, and appear to be gliding through the sky: Henri's back straight, his hand moving forward on the grip of his paddle, his dark knitted cap on his head, his profile French and aquiline; Warren under the bright tumble of hair, his back bending. Their canoe was alive in the forest only months ago, and now on the lake it is a miracle of beauty, of form and symmetry, of dark interstitial seams in mottled abstractions of bark. The time is the present, of course—effectively, and importantly, now—yet without changing a grain of the picture this could be the century before, or the century before that, or the century when the whites first came here in Indians' bark canoes. Two straight wakes trace the way in silence toward the southern end of the lake.

The silence, after a time, is torn apart by a congress of loons: ten loons, racing in circles on the surface of the water, screaming, splashing, squealing like dogs, taxiing in long half-flying runs. For a full ten minutes they keep it up—a ritual insanity, a rampant dance of madness, a convincing demonstration that every one of them is as crazy as a loon.

The long carry has about every obstacle a carry can have, short of German shepherds trained to kill. It has quagmires, slicks of rock, small hills, down trees, low branches, and, primarily, distance. Three miles, even on flat ground, is a long way. In sheer ooze and muck, this portage is as wretched as the Mud Pond Carry. Warren departs first, with a large pack and the tent, to cross, return, and cross again—nine miles. Moving alone, he escapes the compass of tension. Mike follows soon after. Henri tells me not to go on my own but to stay back with Rick and guide and help him. "Stay close to Rick. . . . Stay with Rick. . . . Help Rick," he keeps saying as the three of us go up the trail. The implication is that Rick may collapse, and this is not lost on Rick, who is tight in the throat but seems all the more determined to carry the canoe the whole distance alone. Henri's canoe weighs sixty pounds, Rick's seventy. It is not the weight but the bulk that brings difficulty.

Light branches of balsam springily push the hulls, staggering the walker beneath. With the slightest stumble, the canoes lurch forward, straining the muscles of the legs, neck, and back.

"Help Rick!"

Henri shows no inclination to move ahead by himself. To them both I call out the story of the terrain: "Watch a hole here! . . . The mud is a foot deep here! . . . Low branches here! . . . Step to the left of this little swamp!"

After a mile, Rick's resolve declines. He doubts if he can make it. He rests his canoe on an overhanging branch and asks me if at the halfway point I will give him my pack basket and other gear and take the canoe from there. With that to look forward to, he moves on.

Henri now steps into mud up to his knee and, with a cry, falls. On the way down, he twists his body and spreads his elbows to cushion—as far as is possible—the canoe. He does not seem to care if he cracks every bone in his body as long as he cracks not a rib of the canoe, which lands on top of him and squashes him into the mud.

He gets up cursing me. The fault is mine. I did not tell him where not to step.

I stay closer to him, the better to guide him. He lifts the canoe, moves on a short distance, then puts the canoe down. His Indian carrying board is hurting his head. "Give me your jacket," he says. I give him my jacket. "Get me some string." From my pocket I give him some cord. Terse, angry, he fashions a pad for his head. At this point, Henri seems frightened and shaken with doubt.

Rick, for his part, seems to be, if anything, stronger. Much of the strain has left his face. His vitality, his endurance seem to rise a bit with each part of Henri that comes unstuck.

Warren passes us, going the other way. It is Warren, really, who is defeating the portage—outwalking, outcarrying everyone else. He tells us we are more than halfway. The news is surprising and tonic. I look to Rick. My turn now? He has no thought of giving up his canoe.

After another half mile of narrating the trail, I have become both restless and guilty. I tell Henri I feel pinned down, leading him through the woods, slowly, while Warren is doing so much of the work.

"Well, I'm carrying my share," Henri answers emphatically. Apparently, he wants to believe it. "Anyways," he adds, "Warren is a backpacker. He likes what he is doing."

Not far from the portage end—two hours after the start— Henri calls a halt at a stream for a drink. I am about to go back to help Warren, but Henri insists that I stay—that it is more important to guide the canoes safely to the end of the carry. Raspberry bushes are in fruit around the stream. At leisure, he eats from them. Now and again, he combs his hair. Rick notices moose tracks, large and fresh. We look around. No moose. Henri finds pin cherries and eats them, too. Twenty minutes go by. Warren by now is in his seventh mile. On his back is one of Henri's packs. The other is clutched in his arms.

Henri is a hero of the portage ends, for at such places we encounter other travellers passing through, and they are generally awestruck by the bark canoes. Henri overcomes his constitutional shyness. He moves in close. He fixes his eyes on one of his elbows and answers questions, quaffs the commentary, until the supply is gone.

"Your canoes look Indian, but you don't."

"Did you make them from a kit?"

"Is that real birch bark?"

"Where do you buy them?"

"They looked too fakey to be fake, so I figured they had to be the real thing."

"I've always thought it was painted on."

"Those are old ones, aren't they? All patched up like that?"

"They don't make them like that anymore."

"Congratulations. That's the best imitation of a birch-bark canoe I've ever seen."

("Our little canoe, so neat and strong, drew a favorable criticism from all the wiseacres among the tavern loungers along the road," wrote Thoreau as he approached the woods.)

Henri seems disappointed at portage ends if no one is there. He is not disappointed now. Six men in plastic canoes arrive to begin the carry.

"Are they real?" one of them asks.

"Do you mind if we look them over?"

"You *made* them?"

"*Really?*"

They, in turn, have something to tell us. In Ciss Stream, which lies between the long portage and Caucomgomoc Lake, they saw, thirty minutes ago, a cow moose. Warren arrives with the packs. We load and go.

Ciss Stream, from the portage to the lake, does not drop one inch, and is a deadwater with meanders so curving that they almost form oxbows. In near silence, we steal around its unending bendings through the sedge. Everything is right. The breeze is toward us. The bends conceal us. And the so-called stream is a bog of dry-ki and water-standing grasses—a phreatophytic meadowland, a magnification of Umbazooksus Stream. Our chances thus seem one in one. Another bend. Another scene. No moose. No moose—just the craggy spars of the dry-ki pointing lifeless into the sky. Thousands of trees, dead a century, fill the swamps here, and they are eerily beautiful, silver gray. The logging dams on Caucomgomoc destroyed them so long ago that they are now thought picturesque, their root structures webbing upward thirty feet above the sedge-meadow plain. People came here and killed these trees, and created this unearthly beauty. Another bend. No moose.

The Survival of the Bark Canoe

A mother merganser races squawking out of the sedge and starts down the stream before the two canoes. Screaming, feigning injury, displaying an awkward wing, she leads us around another bend. She will not give up. She will not shut up. She keeps her position, about a hundred feet in front of the canoes, for fully half a mile, raucous all the way. She wrecks the mooselook for good and all. At last, she rises flippantly into the air and flies back to her chicks where she left them.

We round the last bend, and swing into Caucomgomoc. It is two miles wide, and we have about six miles to go—to its far, northwestern corner. Coming directly at us across the lake are the highest waves we have seen yet, driven by a western wind. Henri, in his own drive for the finish, moves straight out onto the water and begins to plow headlong for the farther shore. His caution—what there was of it on Eagle and Chamberlain—is gone. To me, it seems a certainty that we are going to swamp, that we will complete the day with a long, slow swim, dragging the canoes to shore. I check my boots, my pack, to make sure they are firmly tied. I am ready to shrug and see what happens. Warren, however, is not. Having absorbed Henri in silence for something like a hundred and fifty miles, he now turns suddenly and shouts at the top of his lungs, "You God-damned lunatic, head for the shore!" The canoes turn, and head for the shore.

We are pinned down for the rest of the afternoon, squatting among boulders, eating chocolate in the wind—watching the whitecaps, the rolling, breaking, spraying waves. Then, with amazing suddenness after the fall of the sun, the wind subsides and dies. The lake becomes still, smooth, a corridor of glass. We venture out, timid, remembering the wind, then forget it and go straight down the middle the last six miles, mirrored as in the early morning, and under cumulus mountains, in alpenglow, scarlet.

As we touch shore, a young couple with a Grumman canoe are preparing to leave, to paddle into the evening to camp who knows where. She grips her paddle as if it were a baseball bat. He instructs her to separate her hands. Practicing paddling, she strokes the air, pulling the blade past her the narrow way. Stepping into the canoe, she sits in the bow seat, ready to go. But the canoe is beached, fifteen feet from the water. She gets out. He shoves it over the gravel. They get in and paddle off. They go down the lake half a mile, then turn around and come back. They have left standing open all the doors of their car, which is covered with fresh white letters: "JUST MARRIED. BUZZ ON."

Henri cuts poles to support both canoes on the rooftop of his car. Fifteen miles down the dirt-and-gravel road, in what is now the black of night, we are blinded by the oncoming headlights of a many-ton truck, a logging truck—the immense, roaring descendant of the West Branch Drive. The lights are so bright that Henri pulls to the side. On and on the truck approaches, an omnivorous machine, swallowing earth and sky. In the blackness, it dominates all—all light, all sound. Suddenly, though, there is another sound, distinct from the engine's churning. The truck is forcing something up the road, something moving in flight before it, that now, within inches of our windows, pounds by. A hoofbeat clatter, a shape as well, a stir of dust, a glimpse of a form, a terrored eye, a spreading rack—a moose. A bull moose.

It is many hours to the end of Maine. The last glimpse of Henri must wait until then. He has—in Greenville, New Hampshire—one final thing to say to Warren, one farewell remark. He says, "Thanks for taking care of the canoe."

A PORTFOLIO OF
THE SKETCHES
AND MODELS OF
EDWIN TAPPAN
ADNEY
(1868–1950)

Edwin Tappan Adney, who died in the year Henri Vaillancourt was born, spent much of his life collecting material on the art of the making of the bark canoe. He was a journalist, a lecturer, and, ultimately, a consultant on Indian lore to the Museum of McGill University, in Montreal. In 1897, he covered the Klondike for *Harper's Weekly,* and three years later he was *Colliers'* man in Nome. For the most part, though, he lived and worked in eastern Canada. Born in Ohio, he had married a New Brunswick Canadian, and eventually he became a Canadian citizen.

When he was twenty, Adney made a birch-bark canoe, under the guidance of a Malecite builder. Writing down the methodology as he learned it, he began the central work of his life —making sketches, making notes, and traveling to Indian outposts to absorb and record both the basic craftsmanship and the differences in tribal styles. He understood Indian languages. The material he assembled, over decades, had not been gathered in anything like such detail and scope before, nor could it ever be again, for in Adney's lifetime the number of makers of bark canoes declined from the thousands to a scattered, vestigial few. Alone, Adney preserved this immemorial technology; but when he died he had—with the exception of a couple of short articles that appeared in 1890 and 1900—published none of it.

The collection, in hundreds of folders in long file boxes, went into a library storeroom in the Mariners Museum, in Newport News, Virginia. Howard Chapelle, who was Curator of Transportation at the Smithsonian Institution, went through Adney's papers and—adding where necessary his own research—published in 1964 *The Bark Canoes and Skin Boats of North America*, the book that became Henri Vaillancourt's vocational college.

What follows here is a selection of Adney's sketches and models, some of which are included in the Adney-Chapelle book. Most are being published for the first time. They are not intended to be a manual on bark-canoe-building (Adney-Chapelle is all of that and more), but merely to suggest in one more way the complexity of the craft—to give the reader a sense of what Adney did, and, through Adney's pen, a sense of what the Indians did for centuries before.

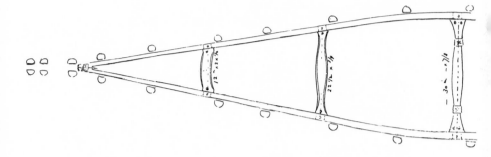

The first seven sketches show the development of a bark canoe from an outline on a building bed to a boat near completion. In this one, stakes have been driven into the ground around the building frame.

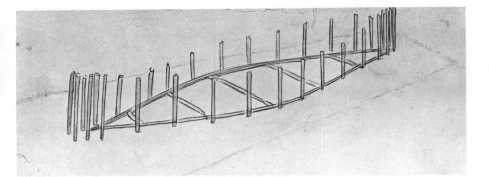

The peripheral lines are not meant to suggest bark, but merely the dimensions of the bed, the carefully chosen and smoothed-out patch of ground where one canoe after another was built—not just for years, but, in some places, for many generations.

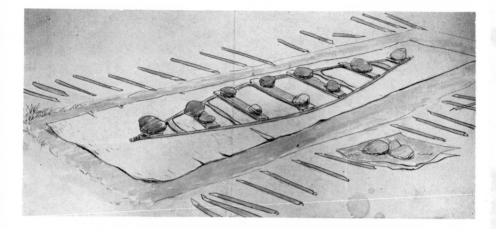

Now the stakes are out and the bark is down. The building frame
—weighted with rocks—has been lined up as accurately as
possible with the stake holes invisible beneath the bark.

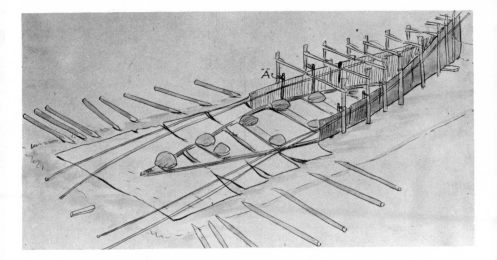

Folding up the bark, the builder gradually replaced the stakes in their holes. Small sticks, tied to the stakes, pinched the bark and held it in place. Without the V-shaped cuts in the bark—known as gores—the bark would not fold properly. Like all seams in the canoe, the gores would be sewn with the split roots of black spruce or white pine. Long strips of cedar—not to remain in the finished canoe—were sometimes (as here) inserted between the small sticks and the bark to influence the fairing of the sides.

Only open / doubled slats / above mower (?) line / Two root ends

The end slats will be pushed into to 45°, and then brought to some position again / holding curved uprights in place

Têtes de Boule. Obas. Pitigway - 1926. Middle from head canoe.

It was rare that any canoe could be covered with bark from a single tree—least of all a great fur-trade canoe, which, in a nascent stage, is the subject of this particular sketch. Fur-trade canoes had high ends, curving back upon themselves with tumblehome; hence extra bark was needed there. Even a relatively small canoe generally had to be "pieced out" with additional bark, one roll being sufficient to cover the ends but not the middle, where the span was considerably greater.

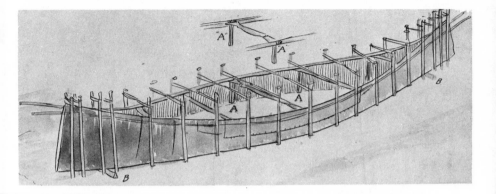

This is a conventional canoe again—about sixteen feet long. The
basic roll of bark has covered the ends. The middle has been
pieced out. The gunwales and thwarts are in place, establishing
the upper profile, or sheer, of the canoe. The bark has, for the
most part, been trimmed, and is ready for lashing to the gunwales.
If the gunwales and thwarts were used as the building frame
around which the bark was folded, the sides of the canoe will
bulge with tumblehome. If the building frame was narrower (a
separate construction, termed by Adney a "false frame"), the
sides of the canoe will flare.

Now the canoe is virtually complete. All seams and gores are sewn. Stempieces (not visible) have been stitched in place to form the ends. A bark deck flap (*wulegessis*) has been laid across the gap at each end where gunwales join, then held in place by the gunwale caps. Cedar planking (in lengths that run from ends to middle) has been arranged as lining to the bark, and is being pressed against the bark by temporary ribs. From the ends, the tapping in of the permanent ribs has begun. They will meet in the middle when the final rib is tapped in, under the center thwart.

Adney tried to miss nothing, as this typical sketch, and its rush of notes, indicates. This is what he came away with after a look at a canoe he had not previously seen—in this case, a "two and a half fathom" Algonquin canoe. (Its overall length was fifteen feet six inches.) Adney's scrawled observations cover everything from the depth of the end stitching to the fact that the ribs of this canoe would be the same as those found in a large Ojibway canoe. The depth of the gores indicated to him that the canoe had been shaped around a false frame.

"Algonquin" Vic. Mus.

1st inspection

see other paper for final measurements

Scale 1/12

More Sheer than others

Scale 1" = 1 foot

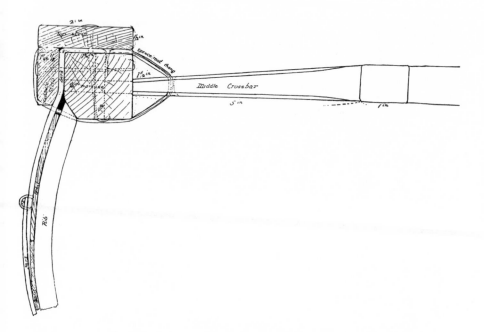

Adney submitted this sketch with an article that was published in *Harper's Young People* in 1890. It shows parts as they fit together at the gunwale. The large block, beveled in one corner, is a sectional view of the inwale, into which is mortised the center thwart, or, as Adney labels it here, the "middle crossbar." The bark comes up between the inwale and the outwale ("outside strip") and is protected from above—as are the root lashings—by the gunwale cap ("top strip"). Between the bark and the rib is the planking. The ringlike configuration to the left of the rib is a bit of split root, sewing two pieces of bark together.

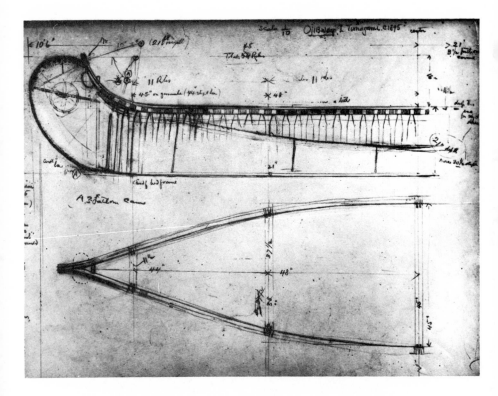

These details of a three-fathom Ojibway canoe nicely show the relationship between ribs and group lashings, which must be discontinuous in order to allow the tips of the ribs to fit into the gunwales.

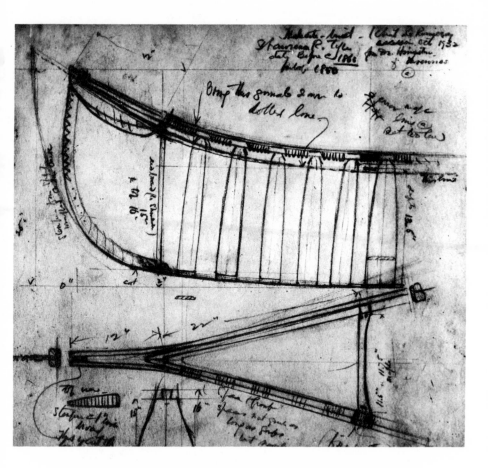

The harplike configuration of the end of the canoe was formed by
the ends of the gunwales, the curving stempiece, and the vertical
headboard (or endboard). The plan-view sketch shows how the
inwales were placed together and held within the outwales.

The relationship of headboard to stempiece is shown more clearly here, in the second and fourth sketches from the left. The headboard took over from the ribs and filled out the narrowest parts of the canoe. The stempiece third from the left best illustrates how stempieces were made. The part that was to be curved was delicately split into many laminations. The rest remained solid wood. After soaking in water, the laminations were bent to a desired curve, then tied in place with basswood bark.

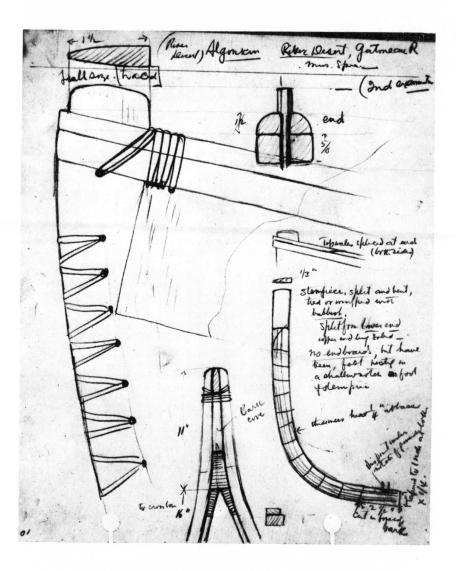

Henri Vaillancourt's canoes do not have protruding stempieces, as does this Gatineau River Algonquin canoe. Note the long laminations of the stempiece, and the lashings of the inwales.

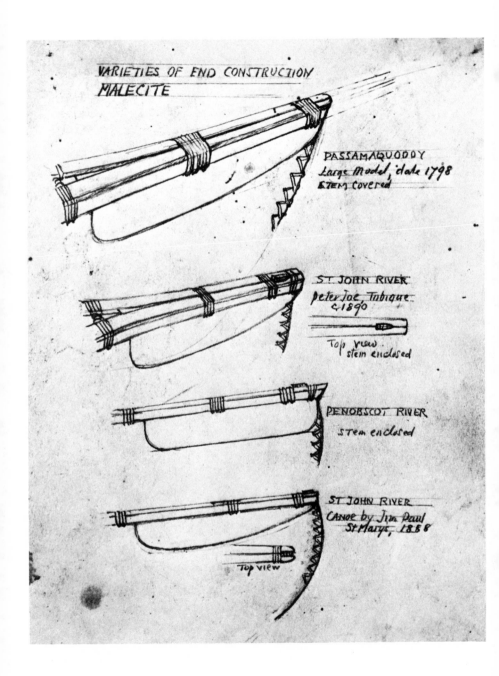

VARIETIES OF END CONSTRUCTION
MALECITE

PASSAMAQUODDY
Large Model, date 1798
STEM Covered

ST JOHN RIVER
peter Joe Tobique
c 1890

Top view.
stem enclosed

PENOBSCOT RIVER
stem enclosed

ST JOHN RIVER
Canoe by Jim Paul
St Marys, 1888

Top view

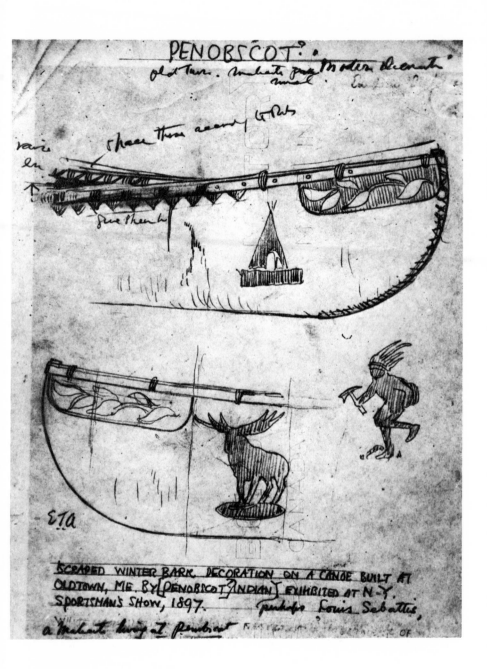

PENOBSCOT?

old Tow. Indicate gray Modern decorat?

SCRAPED WINTER BARK DECORATION ON A CANOE BUILT AT OLDTOWN, ME. BY [PENOBSCOT?] INDIAN] EXHIBITED AT N.Y. SPORTSMAN'S SHOW, 1897. perhaps Louis Sabattis,

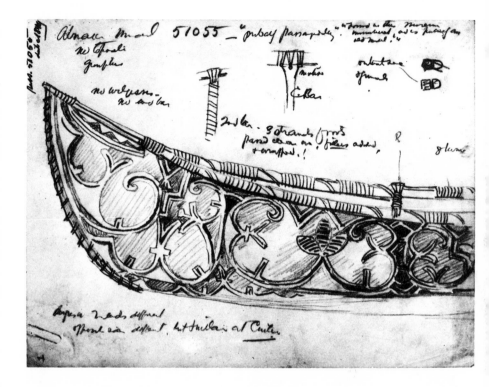

The inside of the bark was the outside of the canoe. Bark removed in winter had a rind in which decorations—sometimes elaborate—could be scraped.

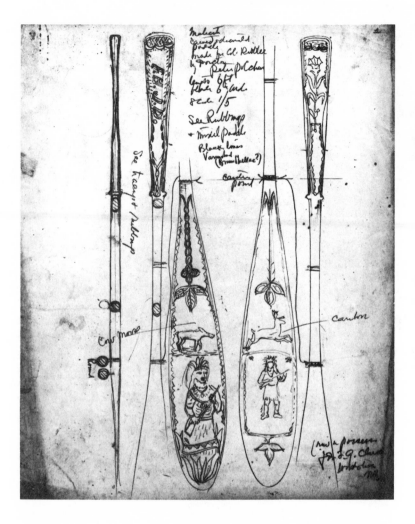

These are Malecite paddles, showing, among other things, a cow moose, a caribou, and rifle-bearing braves. Henri Vaillancourt, decorating his own paddles, usually follows simpler designs: a moose here and there, vine leaves covering the blade and the grip.

P's-tā!k'n "Canoe Shoes" — Malacite
New Brunswick

Malecite Canoe Shoes.
Thin cedar splits, strung on Ash splints, tied to
Bottom of Canoe, for rough, wavy streams used
when going down stream
1893

Bark canoes lasted ten years, in part because they were tough and in part because they were respected. Here is an inventive Malecite idea. Slats, collectively called "canoe shoes," were tied onto canoes' bottoms as fenders against rocks in rapids.

The Micmac Rough-Water Canoe (above) was built for use on, among other places, the ocean. It could be rigged for sail. For portaging, the Algonquin Gatineau River Canoe (opposite) was equipped with reinforcing bars. The sketch also exemplifies clearly the way a midsection was generally pieced out. Note the differences between the profiles of its ends and those of the Ojibway canoe below it.

3 Bars newfound

Ojibway large canoe at Mattawa Ottawa River 27th 1897

Adney kept his records with models, too. He was an accomplished builder who had once made military-equipment training models for the Canadian army, and his model canoes were beautiful studies in precision and form—complex, detailed, in every way reflecting the art they copied. He built well over a hundred, from many tribes and styles. Most were between two and three feet long. He built a fur-trade-canoe model that was over seven feet. Unlike the silly boats that come out of northland roadside shops, his models were—of the ages they represented—authentic souvenirs. A selection of fifteen follows. All are in Newport News, at the Mariners Museum, where—it is hoped—some of Henri Vaillancourt's canoes will one day be collected, too.

An Ojibway four-thwart rice-harvesting canoe.

The Naskapi Crooked Canoe—built of many pieces of bark, because birches are small where these canoes were made, near Hudson Bay.

The Chipewyan Mackenzie River Canoe.

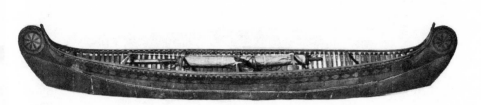

A Têtes de Boule canoe.

The Micmac Woods Canoe—with the personal mark of Old Joe Pictou (the crescent moon).

Iroquois hickory-bark canoe. Where birches were inadequate or unavailable, other barks could be used—but not for much more than crossing a river.

Cree.

Montagnais.

Canot de Maître—a six-fathom, fur-trade, birch-bark canoe.
Cargo: four tons. The white spirals and rayed figures painted on
the ends were copied by Indians from designs of European
immigrants and are related to the rayed discs that still appear on
Pennsylvania Dutch barns.

Among canoes of all tribes and styles, the ones that most attracted
Adney were the varied canoes of the Malecites. The tribe lived
in New Brunswick and parts of Maine, in the center of the
terrain where the best white birches grew. In a Malecite canoe—
the bark ones, anyway—beauty and function each came through
at very high levels, and in balance. This one, of origins in eastern
Maine, was a typical Malecite river canoe.

And this was a Malecite racing canoe.

And this was a Malecite moosehide canoe—ninety-nine per cent
function and one per cent form.

The sharp, pointed ends of this Malecite were ancient in design.

Finally, these two. They are both Malecite canoes; and they are the kind Henri Vaillancourt most often builds. They look much like the pair we traveled in through the woods of Maine. This one is the St. Lawrence River Canoe.

And this is the St. John River Canoe.